The Kids' Knitting Notebook

Cindy Craig

A LARK/CHAPELLE BOOK
A Division of Sterling Publishing Co., Inc.
New York

W9-CFB-861

SCHAUMBURG TOWNSHIP DISTRICT LIBRARY
JUVENILE DEPT.
130 SOUTH ROSELLE ROAD
SCHAUMBURG, ILLINOIS 60193

Editor: Veronika Alice Gunter

Technical Editor: K. J. Hay

Art Director: Robin Gregory

Photographer: John Widman

Illustrator: Orrin Lundgren

Art Production Assistant:
Bradley Norris

Editorial Assistance:
Rose McLarney

A Lark/Chapelle Book

Chapelle, Ltd., Inc.
P.O. Box 9255, Ogden, UT 84409
(801) 621-2777 • (801) 621-2788 Fax
e-mail: chapelle@chapelleltd.com
Web site: www.chapelleltd.com

3 1257 01791 0281

Library of Congress Cataloging-in-Publication Data

Craig, Cindy.
  The kids' knitting notebook / Cindy Craig. -- 1st ed.
    p. cm.
  Includes index.
  ISBN 1-60059-063-2 (hardcover)
  1. Knitting--Juvenile literature. 2. Knitting--Patterns--Juvenile
literature. I. Title.
  TT820.C8562 2007
  746.43'2041--dc22

                          2006032448

10 9 8 7 6 5 4 3 2 1

First Edition
Published by Lark Books, A Division of Sterling Publishing Co., Inc., 387 Park Avenue
South, New York, NY 10016

Text © 2007, Cindy Craig
Photography and Illustrations © 2007, Lark Books

Distributed in Canada by Sterling Publishing,
c/o Canadian Manda Group, 165 Dufferin Street, Toronto, Ontario, Canada M6K 3H6

Distributed in the United Kingdom by GMC Distribution Services, Castle Place, 166
High Street, Lewes, East Sussex, England BN7 1XU

Distributed in Australia by Capricorn Link (Australia) Pty Ltd., P.O. Box 704, Windsor,
NSW 2756 Australia

If you have questions or comments about this book, please contact:
Lark Books, 67 Broadway, Asheville, NC 28801 (828) 253-0467

Manufactured in China

ISBN 13: 978-1-60059-063-4
ISBN 10: 1-60059-063-2

For information about custom editions, special sales, premium and corporate
purchases, please contact Sterling Special Sales Department at 800-805-5489
or specialsales@sterlingpub.com.

The Kids' Knitting Notebook

Your Knitting Notebook

Did you thumb through this book and find oodles of cool projects you want to make? Can you see yourself wearing the flirty mini-sweater on page 102? How about the chic holster on page 85 for your phone or MP3 player? Would your best friend flip for those personalized flip-flops on page 80, or a fringed poncho like the one on page 97? Maybe you've already decided to create every one of the 27 knits, plus their variations. I'd better hurry up and explain how to use this book so you can get started!

I wrote this book so you could have a great introduction to knitting. It's a one-of-a-kind notebook to use to make fun and fabulous projects AND to scrapbook your new life as a knitter. The step-by-step instructions are clear and simple so you can do it all yourself. Plus, you get special places to scribble your thoughts, ideas, and doodles. Notice the dividers and the pocket at the back for photographs and swatches. You can flip through your notebook anytime to see pictures of you and your friends and family modeling the handmade knits you've made.

Here's what you'll find in your knitting notebook:

 Check-offs There's one check-off box for each and every step of the project instructions. When you finish a step, check the box, color it in—whatever you want. That way you'll never lose your place, even if you need to take a break.

Journaling You'll have journal space to write about what you want to knit, who you're knitting for, or anything else you're thinking. Each space includes an idea to get you started.

 Picture Place Here's where you can tape photographs of what you've made—maybe even snapshots from a knitting slumber party. Each Picture Place includes a suggestion for what to photograph.

 Swatch Watch A swatch is the practice piece you knit before you actually start your project. (You'll find out more about making a swatch later.) Save your swatches, needles, or anything else you want in the Swatch Watch pockets throughout this book.

When's the last time you got to write in a book? Gather your coolest pens in your favorite colors. It's your knitting notebook—enjoy it!

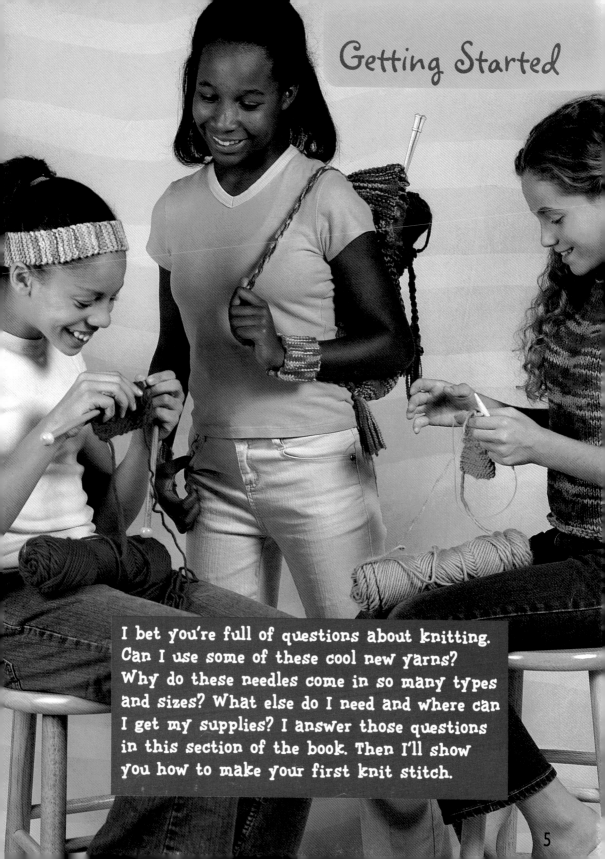

I bet you're full of questions about knitting. Can I use some of these cool new yarns? Why do these needles come in so many types and sizes? What else do I need and where can I get my supplies? I answer those questions in this section of the book. Then I'll show you how to make your first knit stitch.

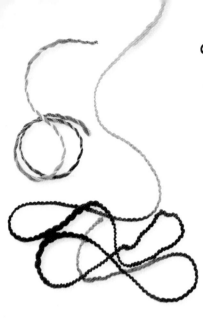

Yarn

Yarn is the material you'll use to knit. It's made from many different fibers, so you have lots of options. The important thing is to choose a yarn that looks and feels right for the project you want to make.

- **Wool:** It's made from the hair of animals, such as sheep, alpacas, and llamas, so whatever you knit with it will keep you warm in cold weather. (Wool has to be washed by hand.)

- **Cotton and linen:** These are lightweight yarns made from plants. They're great for projects that are meant to keep you cool. They also come in all sorts of colors. (You can usually wash these yarns in a machine.)

- **Novelty yarns:** Think polyester. Accessories or clothing made from these **synthetic** (artificial) fibers, such as acrylic, nylon, microfiber, or polyamide, are soft and stretchy. And they can be worn year-round. (They're also easy to wash.)

- **Blended yarns:** Want to mix it up and save some cash? Yarns made from a combination of different fibers, such as something that's 50% wool and 50% acrylic, are cheaper but have just as many color choices as the others. Beginning knitters use a lot of yarn, so why not start with something that won't eat up all of your allowance? (Read the label for washing instructions.)

Balls, Skeins & Hanks

Yarn is sold in **balls**, **skeins** (rhymes with rains), or **hanks**. Balls and skeins are often grouped together on store shelves but they're different. Yarn balls look like flattened balls. They're magnets for cats, dogs, and baby brothers and sisters looking for a toy. Skeins are oblong and not as much fun to roll around. Yarns prepared in balls and skeins are ready to use. Just find the end to get started.

Hanks of yarn resemble twisted pretzels. Think of them as handfuls of yarn. If you don't wind this yarn into a ball before you get started, you'll have a huge mess. So undo the twist of yarn and find the big loop. Have a friend hold the loop open or hang it over the edge of a chair. Find one end of the yarn and wind it into a ball. Then the yarn is ready to use.

Yarn Weights

Yarn comes in many different thicknesses, called **weights**. Most of the projects in this book are made with yarns that are pretty fat. Knitting with fat yarns usually means you finish your project sooner than if you were to use thin yarns. Beginning knitters like to start with fat yarns because they're easier to hold in their hands. It's the same as those fat crayons you used in kindergarten before you could use the skinny ones. The chart below shows you the different weights of yarn, the types (names) of yarns, the average **gauge** for each weight, and the needle size usually used with each weight. (Read more about gauge on page 17.)

Yarn weight & symbol	Types of yarn in category	Number of stitches in 4 inches (10 cm)	Recommended US needle size
Super Fine (1)	Baby, Fingering, Sock	27-32	1-3
Fine (2)	Sport, Baby	23-26	3-5
Light (3)	DK, Light Worsted	21-24	5-7
Medium (4)	Worsted, Afghan, Aran	16-20	7-9
Chunky (5)	Chunky, Craft, Rug	12-15	9-11
Super Chunky (6)	Bulky, Roving	6-11	11 and up

Reading Yarn Labels

From just looking at a yarn's **label**, you can find out:

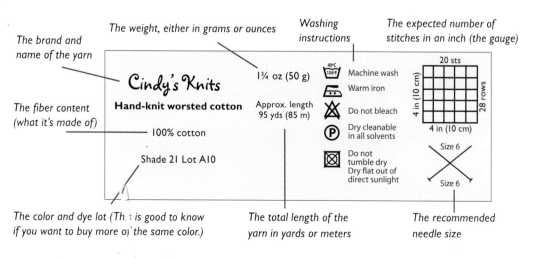

The brand and name of the yarn

The weight, either in grams or ounces

Washing instructions

The expected number of stitches in an inch (the gauge)

Cindy's Knits

1¾ oz (50 g)

Machine wash

Warm iron

Hand-knit worsted cotton

Approx. length 95 yds (85 m)

Do not bleach

The fiber content (what it's made of)

100% cotton

Dry cleanable in all solvents

20 sts

4 in (10 cm)

28 rows

Shade 21 Lot A10

Do not tumble dry
Dry flat out of direct sunlight

4 in (10 cm)

Size 6

Size 6

The color and dye lot (This is good to know if you want to buy more of the same color.)

The total length of the yarn in yards or meters

The recommended needle size

Where to Buy Yarn

Buy from the place with the best selection, of course. A yarn shop! Great knitters tend to work, shop, and teach there. That's important because knitters make friends fast, and they'll help you find what you need and answer your questions. The yarn shop might even have a knitting group you can join. Check your phone book under "yarn" or "knitting." You could also shop at a craft store or department store. With a parent's permission, you can find yarn for sale on the Internet.

My Local Yarn Shops...

Name	Phone number	Website

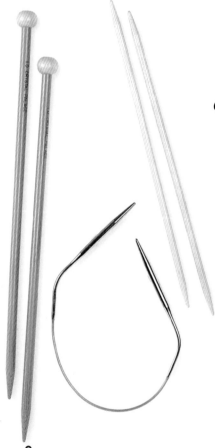

Knitting Needles

Knitting needles come in all different shapes, materials, and sizes. They usually come in pairs—and you need both needles to knit. (Circular needles are the exception, because they are attached.) So take the time to find needles that are right for your project. Buy the ones that feel the most comfortable in your hands.

Shapes

- **Straight needles** are traditional knitting needles. They're ideal for straight or flat projects, such as I Want That Headband on page 26, the Cuddle Bear on page 34, and the Music & Movies Tote on page 63.

- **Circular needles** are straight knitting needles connected by a wire. You can use them for all kinds of knitting. They're ideal for knitting tube-shaped projects, like the Rompin' Round Hat on page 87. Circular needles are also handy for projects that have lots of stitches on the needle at one time, like the Follow-the-Rainbow Scarf on page 54. They are my favorite type of needle.

- **Double pointed needles** have points at both ends—like a pencil sharpened at both ends. This type of needle is used for knitting small circles or tubes. I used these needles at the top of the Happy Hat on page 56, where the top of the hat is smaller than the bottom.

Materials

There are metal needles, plastic needles, and wooden ones. You can even find knitting needles made out of bamboo wood, which are perfect for beginners. They're lightweight, easy to handle, easy to use with all kinds of yarns, and they're inexpensive. Whatever you choose, be sure to keep your knitting needles together. You can't knit with a single needle!

Sizes

Knitting needles can as be as narrow as a toothpick or as wide as a broomstick. The width determines the size, and knitting needles come in whole and half sizes, just like shoes.

The larger the number, the thicker the needle. The projects in this book call for sizes ranging US #9 to US #13. (The metric equivalents, 5.5 mm to 9 mm, are a measurement of the needle's diameter.)

Notions & Other Knitting Stuff

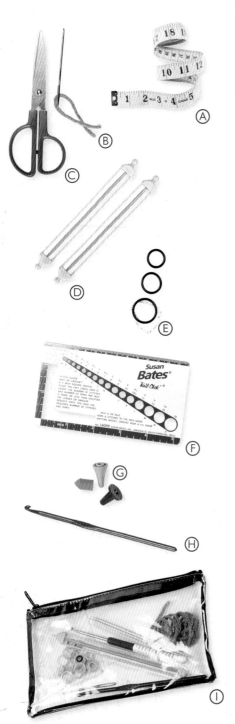

Tools that knitters use regularly are called **notions**. That's basically everything other than yarn and knitting needles. Each project pattern in this book includes a What You Need list, so you can collect all the items on the list before you get started. Here are some common notions:

- **Tape measure:** A flexible tape measure works well. The retractable ones are nice because they don't get tangled in your yarn. Ⓐ

- **Tapestry needle (yarn needle):** Look for a blunt tip needle (instead of a sharp tip). Choose one with a large eye (opening at the top) for the yarn to pass through. A tapestry needle with a bent tip works great. Ⓑ

- **Scissors:** If they can cut the yarn, they'll work. You can use craft scissors. Ⓒ

- **Stitch holder:** These hold your stitches on your needle. Get double-ended holders if you can; they work best. Ⓓ

- **Stitch markers:** These are small, colored rings that you slip on your knitting needle to remind you to do something special or to help you count stitches. Ⓔ

- **Needle gauge:** This nifty gadget has holes in it. You stick unmarked knitting needles into the holes to figure out their sizes. Ⓕ

- **Point protectors:** When you're on the go and not yet finished with your project, slide these on the tips of your needles to keep your stitches on the needles. Ⓖ

- **Crochet hook:** A tool for attaching fringe, fixing mistakes, and more. A size J is good for most uses. Ⓗ

- **Small zipper bag:** You'll need to keep your supplies organized. Use a small zipper bag or a pencil case. Ⓘ

- **Tote bag:** Many knitters choose to keep your projects and supplies together in a special bag. A tote bag works great.

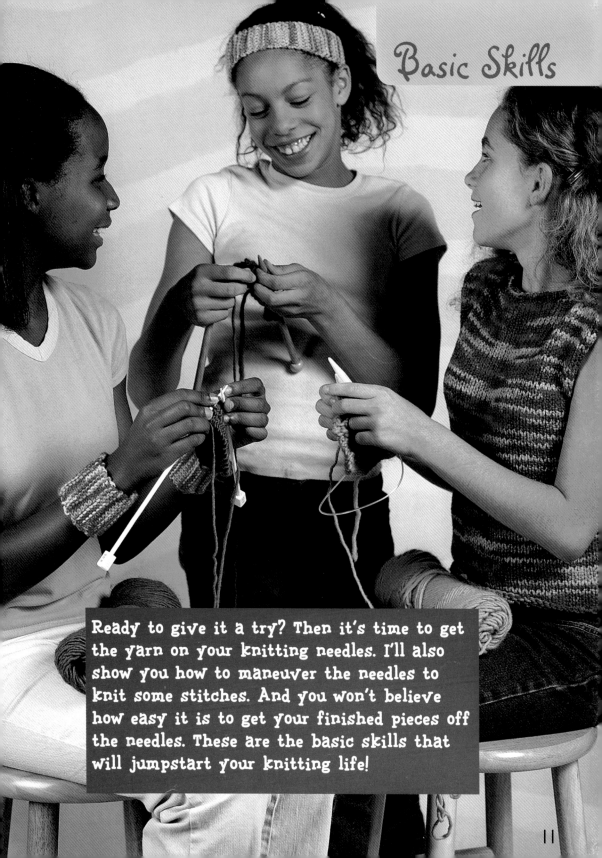

Ready to give it a try? Then it's time to get the yarn on your knitting needles. I'll also show you how to maneuver the needles to knit some stitches. And you won't believe how easy it is to get your finished pieces off the needles. These are the basic skills that will jumpstart your knitting life!

CO	Cast On
K	Knit
St	Stitch
Sts	Stitches
BO	Bind Off
K2tog	Knit two together
Kf&b	Knit in front & back of stitch
PM	Place stitch marker
P	Purl stitch
P2tog	Purl two together
St St	Stockinette stitch
YO	Yarn over

The Code

In most knitting books, the instructions for a project (the pattern) use abbreviations for common techniques. It keeps the directions nice and short. For instance, the **casting on** technique I'm about to show you appears as "CO." The code for stitch is "st," and the code for stitches is "sts."

To help you learn this knitting lingo, I'll use the knitting terms, followed by the code in parentheses, the first time a technique is used in a set of project instructions. After that, I'll only use the code.

Cast On

In case you hadn't guessed by now, knitting is all about connecting loops of yarn. Each loop is called a **stitch**. The **cast on** puts the starting stitches on your needle. (That's why some people call the cast on the "starter row.") Casting on is usually the first step in any project pattern. There are many different ways to cast on. I think the easiest one to learn is the **long tail** cast on.

You'll need smooth, worsted weight yarn (see page 7 for the Yarn Weights Chart) and a single needle. Select a needle size recommended on the yarn label. If there is no label, use a needle that is a little larger than the thickness of your yarn. You'll use about 1 inch (2.5 cm) of yarn for each stitch you create, so make sure you have about an arm's length of yarn to practice this skill.

(A)

(B)

(C)

1. Hold the needle in your right hand. Use your left hand to lay about 12 inches (30.5 cm) of the yarn over the needle (this is the long tail and should hang behind the needle). Hold the yarn in place on the needle with the index finger of your right hand. (A)

2. Pinch the thumb and index finger of your left hand together and reach between the two strands of yarn hanging down on either side of the needle. (B)

3. With the rest of the fingers of your left hand, hold both ends of the yarn against the palm of your hand, about 4 inches (10 cm) below the needle. Spread your thumb and index finger apart, separating the strands of yarn. (C)

4. Rotate your left hand toward you, so you are looking at the palm of your hand. Bring the needle down and toward you, drawing the yarn between your thumb and index finger. You'll now see the yarn making a V between your thumb and index finger, like a slingshot. Ⓓ

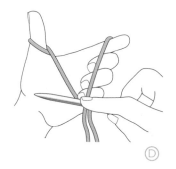

5. Insert the tip of the needle under the strand of yarn wrapped around your thumb.

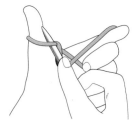

6. Move the tip of the needle to the right, in front of the yarn on your index finger. Then slide the needle under that yarn, moving the tip right to left. Ⓕ

7. Draw that strand of yarn on your index finger down and to the left, all the way through the loop on your thumb. Ⓖ

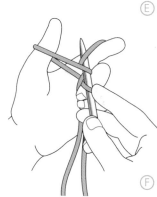

8. Take your left thumb out of its loop.

9. Now the loop's on your needle. Tighten the loop by pulling down on both tails. The front tail will move more than the back one. Do you see two loops of yarn on your needle? You should. That means you've cast on two stitches. Congratulations! Ⓗ

10. Practice casting on. (After the initial cast on, you'll notice that each new cast on adds just one stitch.) Just repeat steps 2 through 9 until you've used up your length of yarn. Got the hang of it?

The Casting On Story

Here's a simple, silly story I teach my friends to say to themselves to remind them how to cast on:

Step 1: Make the tent

Step 2: Pincher fingers go in the tent

Step 3: Grab the tiger tails

Step 4: Look at your palm and make a sling shot

Step 5: Bunny goes up the hole

Step 6: And around the tree

Step 7: And down the hole

Step 8: And the hole closes up

Step 9: Tug the tiger tails

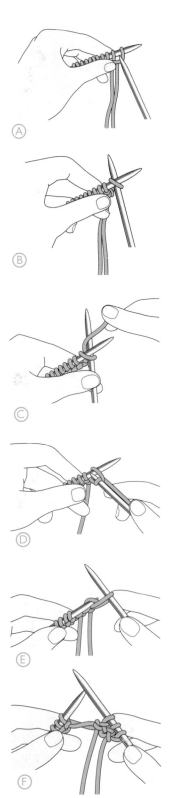

The Knit Stitch

The **knit stitch** is the technique used to make every project in this book. Lucky for you, it's easy to learn.

You'll need smooth, worsted weight yarn and a pair of needles. (See page 7 for the Yarn Weights Chart.) Select a needle size that is recommended on the yarn label. If there is no label, use a needle that is a little larger than the thickness of your yarn. You'll want to practice the knit stitch a lot, so make sure you have at least 20 yards (18 m) of yarn.

1. Cast on about 15 stitches. Hold the needle in your left hand so that the knots of the cast on stitches are on the bottom.

2. Place the tip of the right needle between the first two stitches on the left needle. (A) Push the tip of the right needle through the first stitch and to the right. The needles will form an X. The right needle should be on the bottom. (B)

3. Grab the **working yarn** with your right hand. (This is the section of yarn being used to knit—not the tail of the cast on.) Bring this yarn up from behind and wrap it right to left (counter-clockwise) around the bottom needle. See how you've pulled the yarn into the center of the X? (C)

4. Move the tip of the right needle down and toward you, under the left needle and out of the stitch. (This movement is opposite to how you put your needle into the stitch.) The right needle's tip should draw the yarn wrap through the stitch. There should be a loop of yarn on your right needle now. (D)

5. Slide the right needle to the right until the first stitch on the left needle moves off the needle. You've just created your first knit stitch! (E)

6. Repeat steps 2 through 5 with each cast-on stitch on your needle. (F) When you finish your row, all the stitches will be on the right needle and your left needle will be empty. Trade hands to begin the new row.

When starting a new row, and before you insert your needle into the first stitch, your working yarn should always be behind the needle and hang straight down.

Garter Stitch

Using the knit stitch in each stitch of every row is called the **garter stitch**. That's what you just did by following the steps on the previous page. If you are told to work six rows of garter stitch, this means that you should work the knit stitch in every stitch for six rows. When you complete the sixth row, you'll notice three horizontal rows on the front and back of the knitted fabric. If you take a closer look, you'll see that the horizontal rows on the backside lie between the horizontal rows on the front side. Each horizontal row is called a **ridge row**.

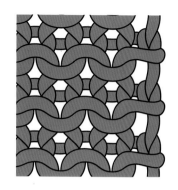

Binding Off

So you've cast on successfully, and you've created knit stitches. But how do you get your project off the knitting needles? That skill is called **binding off** (it's also known as **casting off**). Binding off also keeps your knits from unraveling. To bind off, you move some stitches up and over other stitches. Think of it as a game of leapfrog.

Here's what you do:

1. Knit 2 stitches. (These will be on your right needle.) (A)

2. Use the left needle tip to move the stitches so the first stitch leaps over the second stitch—and off the right needle. (B) (Some people use the left needle to move the stitches and some people use their fingers. Do what's easiest for you.) You'll see that you have one stitch on the right needle. (C)

3. Knit the next stitch.

4. Repeat steps 2 and 3. (D)

5. Cut the yarn about 10 inches (25 cm) from your work so it looks like a tail.

6. Lift the right needle up so it stretches the last loop on your needle until the tail pulls all the way through the last stitch. That's it! You've completed a nice bind off.

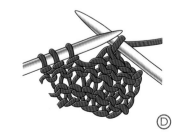

15

Weaving In Ends

You've cast on, made knit stitches, and even done the binding off of your test pieces. What's left to do? Well, you have at least two ends of yarn to hide, don't you? One end is where you began working; the other is where you finished. Hiding these yarn ends is called **weaving in**. Hiding your ends makes your work look more complete. Because weaving in literally takes care of all the loose ends, this technique can reduce the chances that your knitting will fall apart.

To practice weaving in, you'll need a piece of knitting with loose ends, a tapestry needle, and scissors.

Ⓐ

1.   Find all the loose ends.

2.   Find the side of your project people won't see (called the wrong side) like the inside of a shirt.

3.   Starting with one loose end, thread it through the eye of a tapestry needle.

4.   Insert the needle under one of the bumps (knit stitches) near that loose end, then up and under the next bump. Ⓐ Continue doing this for about 2 inches (5 cm) worth of bumps. If your project is smaller than 2 inches (5 cm), work the tail through more rows.

5.   Working in the opposite direction, insert the needle under the bumps on the next row.

6.   Cut the remaining yarn about 1 inch (2.5 cm) away from your work.

7.   Repeat steps 3 through 6 until all ends are woven into the hidden side of your project. Now doesn't that look better?

Journaling

There are so many knitting needles to choose from! And even more yarns!

So far I've used... ....

but I might try... ....

Make a Practice Piece

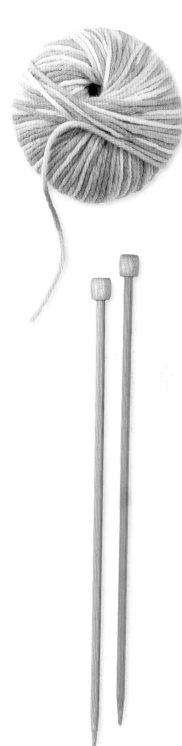

Everything you knit should function as fantastically as it looks. So in my patterns, I let you know which projects require a **swatch**. (This is also called a **practice piece**.) A swatch is just a small section of knitted fabric that shows how many stitches should be created per inch of knitting. (That's the **gauge**.) If you're making the Envelope Purse on page 42, you want lots of stitches per inch (cm). That means you'll knit tightly enough so that your keys and money won't fall out of the finished purse. If you're making a lightweight scarf that should softly wrap around your neck like the one on page 28, you want a loose knit. So you'll create fewer stitches per inch. The needle you use, the type of yarn, and the unique way you knit all add up to determine how tight a piece of knitting will be.

You'll need smooth, worsted weight yarn, a pair of knitting needles (see page 7 for the Yarn Weights Chart), plus scissors, a tape measure, a calculator or good division skills, and a pencil. Write your results on this page. Yeah, right here on the page!

1. Cast on 20 stitches.

2. Knit until your piece measures 4 inches (10 cm) long.

3. Bind off all the stitches.

4. Use a ruler to measure the width of your knitted piece.
(Make your note here ———. Change partial inches into fractions ———.)

5. Complete this equation to calculate the number of stitches in one inch: 20 stitches ÷ ——— inches (cm) = ——— stitches per inch (cm). The number of stitches per inch (cm) is called the gauge.

Swatch Watch

Look at the chapter dividers to find handy pockets.
You can save your swatches there!

Test how the needle size affects gauge. Select another knitting needle that is at least two sizes smaller or larger than the one you used for the first swatch.

1. Cast on 20 stitches.

2. Knit until your piece measures 4 inches (10 cm).

3. Bind off all the stitches.

4. Use a ruler to measure the width of your knitted piece. (Make your note here _____ . Change partial inches into fractions _____ .)

5. Complete this equation to calculate the number of stitches in one inch: 20 stitches ÷ _____ inches (cm) = _____ stitches per inch (cm).

You've learned the basic skills you'll use to knit most of the projects in this book. Way to go! If you make any mistakes, laugh about them. Then turn to page 106 to see how to fix common "uh-ohs." Have fun knitting!

Journaling

I've knitted my first stitches! And I've created my first swatch! The types of projects I'd like to try knitting are...

....

....

....

....

....

....

Stripes, Fringe & More

Why not make a collage of photos, yarns, and whatnot?

Picture Place

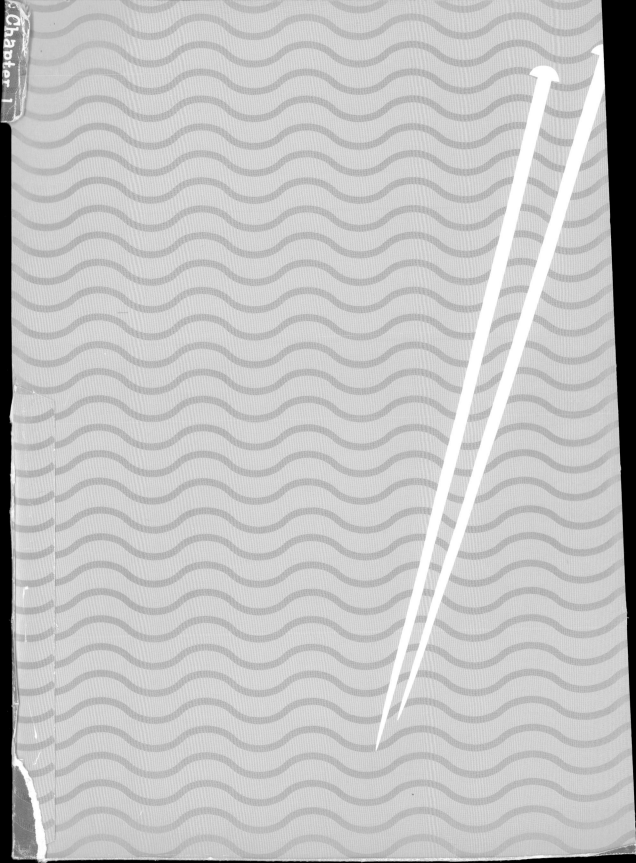

Stripes, Fringe & More

You'll knit all kinds of fun, stylish, and handy projects using the basic skills from the previous chapter. But what if you want to change colors to make stripes? Or add fringed edges? I'll show you how to do that and more on the next few pages. Give these techniques a try when you make the projects you see on this page. The project patterns begin on page 24.

Joining Yarn

If your project uses more than one color or more than one ball of yarn—and a lot of projects do—you'll want to know how to stop using the old yarn and start using the new yarn. That's called **joining yarn**. To give it a try, gather a new ball of smooth, worsted weight yarn, plus several other pieces of smooth, worsted weight yarn, at least 2 yards (2 m) of each. (See page 7 for the Yarn Weights Chart.) You'll also need a pair of needles and scissors. (Select a needle size that is recommended on the yarn label. If there is no label, use a needle that is a little thicker than your yarn.)

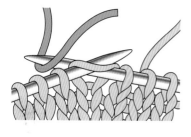

(A)

1. Work until it is time to change the yarn; stop using the old yarn when you have at least 10 inches (25 cm) of yarn remaining.

2. Fold the new yarn about 10 inches (25 cm) from the end.

3. Start the stitch by inserting the right needle into the next stitch on the left needle.

4. Place the fold on the right needle. Continue to hold the folded yarn in your right hand. (A)

5. Complete the stitch.

6. Create your next stitch and make sure to wrap with the working end of the yarn. Keep knitting until it is time to change again. This will leave a small space and a loose stitch where you changed yarns.

7. Hide the space when you hide the two tails. Some people tie a knot here to keep the two tails together.

You'll use the joining yarn technique in the very first project—the Fuzzy Fringed Bookmark on page 24. It uses three to five different yarns.

Fringe

Fringe is a fun finishing touch. To make some, grab a piece of card-board that measures about 12 inches (30.5 cm) wide, any kind of yarn, scissors, a size J crochet hook, and a project that you want to finish with fringe.

1. Wrap the yarn around the cardboard to get the number of fringe pieces the pattern says you'll need. Cut all the strands of the wrapped yarn along one edge of the cardboard. (A)

2. Gather the number of pieces you'll need to fringe one edge of your project. Fold them in half.

3. Find the spot for the fringe. Then insert the crochet hook from the back of the project to the front.

4. Place the fold of one piece of fringe yarn into the crook of the crochet hook.

5. Use the crochet hook to pull the fold halfway through your knitting so the fold, or loop, of the fringe yarn is on the back of the project and the tails are on the front. (B)

6. Thread the tails through the loop and pull to tighten. (C)

7. Repeat steps 4 through 6 to attach the remaining pieces of fringe yarn all along the edge.

8. Repeat steps 3 through 7 for the remaining edges.

9. Give the fringe a haircut, trimming the ends of the fringe evenly with your scissors. Voilà! Fabulous fringe.

(A)

(B)

(C)

A single fringe in a row of fringes is usually made with more than one piece of yarn, sometimes even more than one color. The Follow-the-Rainbow Scarf on page 54 uses six different colors of yarn for fringe.

Whip Stitch

Some of the things you'll knit will be ready to wear as soon as you finish knitting. Other projects will be knit in pieces and then sewn together. The **whip stitch** is a very simple way to sew knitted pieces together. To try this, grab two pieces of knitting that you wish to sew together, yarn that matches the yarn in your project (about 2 inches [5 cm] of yarn per inch of seam), a tapestry needle, and scissors. Make sure that you have enough matching yarn to sew all the seams.

(A)

1. Place the "right" sides of your work together so your knitting is inside out. (The right side is the side you want people to see.)

2. Thread the first 3 inches (7.5 cm) of the sewing yarn through the eye of the tapestry needle.

3. Starting at a corner, insert the needle from the back straight up through both pieces of knitting.

4. Grab the needle and pull the yarn through until you have a 10-inch (25-cm) tail left underneath.

5. Take the needle over the edge of the two layers and insert it again from the back to the front, a short distance from the last stitch. Grab the needle and pull it toward you.

6. Repeat step 5 all along the edge. (A)

7. When you get to the end, trim and weave in the ends of the sewing yarn.

Using a Stitch Holder

Sometimes, to get just the right shape, you'll only knit part of the stitches in a row. That's because you'll come back to finish them later. But you'll need to take the stitches off the needle, and you don't want them to unravel, right? Right. A stitch holder comes in handy to mark those stitches and hold onto them. You just have to remember to close the stitch holder around the stitch!

When the directions in a project pattern tell you to return to those stitches, just put the stitches on the left needle and get back to knitting. Or knit them directly from the holder.

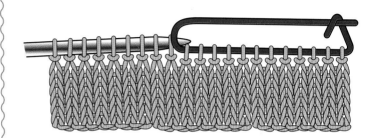

Journaling

Okay—it's time to turn the page and start making my first knitting projects.
Am I feeling nervous, excited—or a little of both?

....

....

....

....

Fuzzy Fringed Bookmark

Mix and match
your favorite yarns
to create a
one-of-a-kind
bookmark.

Size
2 inches (5 cm) wide
and 6 inches (15 cm) t

What You Need
- 5 yards (4.5 m) 3 to
  different yarns of an
  weight
- Knitting needles size
  US #11 (8 mm)
- Scissors

Gauge
Doesn't matter for th
project

Skills You'll Us
- Cast On (page 12)
- Knit Stitch (page 14)
- Joining Yarn (page 20
- Bind Off (page 15)

What You Do

1. As you knit, each row will add to the width of the bookmark. Cast on (CO) 20 stitches (sts) for the length.

2. Knit (K) 1 row.

3. Cut the yarn, leaving a 4-inch (10-cm) tail.

4. To make a new stripe, change your yarn and K 1 row. Cut the yarn, leaving a 4-inch (10-cm) tail.

5. Repeat step 4 until the piece is 2 inches (5 cm) wide or as wide as you would like. Use as many colors as you like.

6. Bind off (BO) all sts.

7. Secure the tails on each end by knotting two pieces together along the edge. If you have an odd number, knot three pieces together at once. One homemade bookmark, at your service.

Journaling

My top 10 favorite books are

1. ....

2. ....

3. ....

4. ....

5. ....

6. ....

7. ....

8. ....

9. ....

10. ....

I Want That Headband

Don't be surprised if a friend borrows this fabulous accessory or asks you to make one for her.

What You Need

40 yards (36.5 m)
worsted weight yarn
(I used Artyarns
Ultramerino 8 #127.)
Knitting needles size
US #9 (5.5 mm)
Tapestry needle

Gauge

stitches = 1 inch (2.5 cm)
garter stitch (knit every
itch in each row)

Skills You'll Use

Cast On (page 12)
Knit Stitch (page 14)
Bind Off (page 15)
Whip Stitch (page 22)
Weave In Ends (page 16)

What You Do

1. You are knitting one piece. The short ends of the piece will be sewn together to form the headband. To start, cast on (CO) 8 stitches (sts).

2. Knit (K) each stitch in every row until the piece measures 15 inches (38 cm) long.

3. Bind off (BO) all sts.

4. Finish the headband by folding it in half so the front sides (the ones you want to show when you are wearing it) are together.

5. Whip stitch the bind-off edge and the cast-on edge together.

6. Weave in the ends. Try on your headband.

This headband uses Artyarns Ultramerino 8 #125 and a handful of fabric rings. Just thread the rings onto your yarn before you get started. Cast on as in step 1. At the beginning of all the remaining rows, slide one of the rings up close to the needle and complete the first stitch. Knit the row as usual. ▶

Journaling

This headband will look great with…

....

....

....

Simple Snuggly Scarf

Count on this neck-nuzzling scarf to surround you with softness and to jazz up an outfit.

Size

6 inches wide by at least 40 inches long (15 cm x 101.5 cm)

What You Need

- 150 yards (137 m) bulky weight yarn (I used Colinette Prism #134 Jamboree.)
- Knitting needles size US #11 (8 mm)
- Scissors
- Tape measure
- Tapestry needle

Gauge

3 stitches = 1 inch (2.5 cm) in garter stitch (knit every stitch in each row)

Skills You'll Use

- Cast On (page 12)
- Knit Stitch (page 14)
- Bind Off (page 15)
- Weave In Ends (page 16)

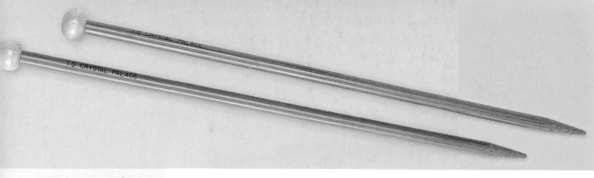

What You Do

1. You are beginning on the bottom edge and will knit the length of the scarf. Cast on (CO) 18 stitches (sts).

2. Knit (K) until your scarf measures 40 inches (101.5 cm) or your desired length.

3. Bind off (BO) all sts.

4. Weave in ends.

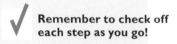 **Remember to check off each step as you go!**

Journal

My first scarf! I knew I could do it, but now that I have my very own made-by-me scarf in my hands I'm thinking ...

....

....

....

....

 ### Picture Place

Why not take a picture of your scarf? Scrapbook it onto the divider at the start of this chapter.

Rah-Rah Striped Scarf

Don't wait for a pep rally to show your school spirit

Size
6 inches (15 cm) wide and 6 inches (153 cm) long, before adding fringe

What You Need
- 175 yards (160 m) bulky weight yarn for main color (I used Brown Sheep Lamb's Pride Bulky Blue Boy.)
- 75 yards (68.5 m) of bulky weight yarn for contrast color (I used Brown Sheep Lamb's Pride M110 Orange You Glad.)
- Knitting needles size US #13 (9 mm)
- Crochet hook size J
- Scissors
- Tape measure
- Tapestry needle

Gauge
2½ stitches = 1 inch (2.5 cm) in garter stitch (knit every stitch in each row)

Skills You'll Use
- Cast On (page 12)
- Knit Stitch (page 14)
- Joining Yarn (page 20)
- Bind Off (page 15)
- Fringe (page 21)

I used Madil Pierrot #317 yarn for the main color and Brazillia Lame #83 yarn for the contrast color on this scarf.

What You Do

1. With your main color, cast on (CO) 150 stitches (sts) very loosely. This will be the length of the knitted part of your scarf. Note: If you cast on tightly, the scarf will curve on one side and might not hang straight.*

2. Knit (K) 6 rows. You're knitting the width of your scarf now.

3. Change to your contrast color. K 4 rows.

4. Change to your main color. K 6 rows.

5. Change to your contrast color. K 4 rows.

6. Change to your main color. K 6 rows.

7. Bind off (BO) all sts loosely.

8. Finish your scarf by adding fringe. Cut 40 pieces from the main color yarn and 40 pieces from the contrasting yarn. Make each fringe using one piece of the main color and one piece of the contrasting color held together. Attach 20 fringes evenly spaced across each end of the scarf.

9. Hide the tails of your color changes by tying them into the fringes. Go team!

* Try casting on with a knitting needle that is one size larger than the needle you plan to use. Start knitting the first row with the needle you will use for the entire project. This will help you have a loose cast-on edge.

Journaling

If I were in charge of things, our school mascot would be...

and our school colors would be...

because...

Beadazzling Belt

Be a trendsetter with this tie-on belt. The beads give it weight, so it will swish and sway as you sashay down the halls at school.

Size
2½ inches wide (6 cm) by as long as you need to tie it loosely around your waist

What You Need
- 120 yards (110 m) worsted weight yarn (I used Cascade Pearls #5420.)
- Knitting needles size US #13 (9 mm)
- Beads, about two handfuls (Make sure the center hole of each bead is big enough so your yarn can go through it. I used clay beads.)
- Crochet hook size J
- Scissors
- Tape measure
- Tapestry needle

Gauge
5 stitches (sts) = 1 inch (2.5 cm) in garter stitch (knit every stitch in each row)

Skills You'll Use
- Cast On (page 12)
- Knit Stitch (page 14)
- Bind Off (page 15)
- Fringe (page 21)
- Weave In Ends (page 16)

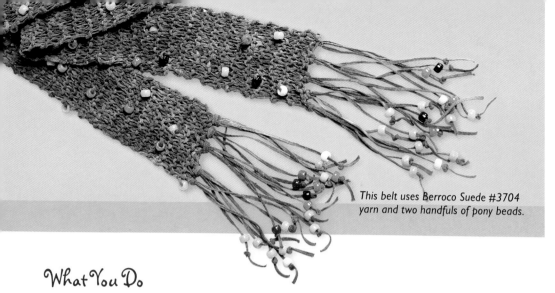

This belt uses Berroco Suede #3704 yarn and two handfuls of pony beads.

What You Do

1. You are beginning at one end of the belt and will knit until the belt is long enough. Thread your tapestry needle with your yarn. String all the beads you plan to use for the entire belt on the yarn before you start knitting.

2. Push the beads back along the yarn as you work. Cast on (CO) 12 stitches (sts).

3. Knit (K) all sts in every row. Randomly push one bead up close to the needle to sit between the stitch you just completed and the next stitch you are about to knit. You might choose to put beads in every row or you might choose to skip a row. It's all up to you.

4. Bind off (BO) when the belt is as long as you like it.

5. To finish your belt, weave in all ends.

6. Add fringe and more beads if you like.

Journal

Knitting with beads was a lot_____than I thought it would be.
If I want to use beads in another project I think I'll...

....

....

....

Cuddle Bear

You're never too old for a teddy bear and who could say no to this adorable one?

Size

10 inches tall (25.5 cm)

What You Need

- 125 yards (114 m) bulky weight yarn for main color (I used Brown Sheep Lamb's Pride Bulky #BM008.)
- 25 yards (23 m) bulky weight yarn for contrast color (I used Brown Sheep Lamb's Pride Bulky #BM029.)
- Knitting needles size US #11 (8 mm)
- Polyester fiberfill
- Ribbon for a bow
- Scissors
- Stitch holder
- Tapestry needle

Gauge

3 stitches = 1 inch (2.5 cm) in garter stitch (knit every stitch of each row)

Skills You'll Use

- Cast On (page 12)
- Knit Stitch (page 14)
- Joining Yarn (page 20)
- Bind Off (page 15)
- Using a Stitch Holder (page 23)
- Whip Stitch (page 22)
- Weave In Ends (page 16)

What You Do

1. Begin by knitting one leg for your bear. Cast on (CO) 6 stitches (sts) and knit (K) 23 rows. You will have 12 ridge rows on one side and 11 on the other for a total of 23 ridges. (See page 00 for more about ridge rows.) Cut your yarn, leaving an 8-inch (20.5-cm) tail and slide this piece to the end of your needle.

2. Now you knit the other leg. CO 6 more sts onto the empty needle. K 23 rows.

3. Move the first section right next to your current section. From this point, you will knit them as one section of 12 sts. This is the beginning of the bear's body.

4. K 7 rows.

5. Now you knit your bear's shirt. Change to your contrasting color. K 16 rows.

6. Time to knit your bear's head. Change to your main color. K 26 rows.

7. Now you knit the other side of your bear's shirt. Change to your contrasting color. K 16 rows.

8. Time to knit the other side of your bear's body. Change to the main color. K 7 rows.

Note: You are about to knit the two leg sections again. In order to do this, some sts will be on a holder until it is time to knit them.

9. K the first 6 sts and place the next 6 sts on a stitch holder.

10. K 23 more rows on the 6 sts remaining on the needle.

11. Bind off (BO) 6 sts.

12. Put the sts from the holder back onto your needle so you can begin knitting your row with the first stitch that is next to the completed leg.

13. Use the main color to K 24 rows.

14. BO 6 sts.

15. Now you make the arms. With your main color, CO 12 sts.

16. K 8 rows.

17. Now you knit the shirt sleeves. Change to your contrast color and K 12 rows.

18. BO 12 sts.

19. Repeat steps 15 through 18 to make another arm.

(continued on next page)

20. To finish your bear, thread your tapestry needle with a piece of your main color yarn. Fold the body piece in half so the legs meet. Beginning at the center of the body where the legs meet, whip stitch down the leg, around the bottom of the foot, and up the side, ending at the fold. Weave in all ends.

21. Thread your tapestry needle with another piece of yarn. Beginning at the body where the legs meet, whip stitch the other leg, around the bottom of the foot, and start up the side. When you get to the color change on the body, stop and stuff the legs with polyester fiberfill.

22. Continue sewing until you have about 1 inch (2.5 cm) left. Fill the rest of the bear with polyester fiberfill. Finish your seam and make a small knot. Slide your needle down the yarn to within 1 inch (2.5 cm) of the bear. Trim the yarn tail to 1 inch (2.5 cm). Wiggle your needle into the bear. Pull out the tip of your needle, leaving the end inside the bear.

23. Fold the arms in half so you have a tube with a stripe of main color (for the bear's paw) and a stripe of contrast color (for the bear's sleeve). Beginning at the fold on the cast-on edge, sew the piece closed. When you get to the edge, turn your work and continue sewing the longer edge. When you get to the top, stuff the arm with polyester fiberfill. Sew the arm to the bear. Repeat for the other arm.

24. To form the ears, thread your tapestry needle with the main color. Pinch the corner where you want the ears. Stitch a straight line. Turn the bear and stitch it again, going the other direction. Make a knot and hide the ends inside the bear. Repeat on the other side.

25. Tie a bow around the neck. Give your bear a hug.

Swatch Watch
Did you create a test piece to check your gauge? You know where to store it!

Shapes & Twisted Cords

Triangle Kerchief

Envy-Me Envelope Purse

Tape a photo here.

This is your scrapbooking space!

Picture Place

Swatch
Pocket

Chapter 2

Shapes & Twisted Cords

Want to knit some fancy shapes? You can. Just reduce the number of stitches in your rows. It's called **decreasing,** and it's easy to do. Use the **knit two together** technique to decrease and make a triangular kerchief and a purse with a flap. The project patterns begin on page 40.

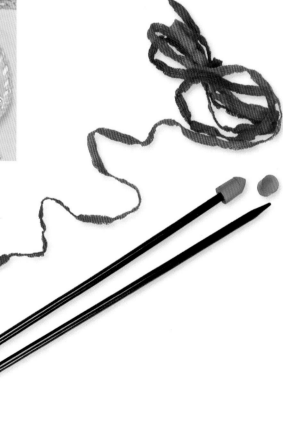

Knit Two Together

You are going to knit two stitches together to create shapes in your knitting. Grab a piece of knitting with the stitches still on the needle and enough yarn to complete at least one more row.

1. Starting at the second stitch on the left-hand needle, insert the tip of the right needle under the front strands of both the second and the first stitch on the left-hand needle.

2. Wrap the yarn around the bottom (right) needle and, with the right needle, draw the yarn through both stitches. Ⓐ

3. Slide the right needle to the right until the second and the first stitches on the left needle move completely off the needle. You've completed your first knit two together.

4. Finish knitting the remaining stitches in the usual way. Count the stitches on your row. Did you notice that you have one less stitch than before? Yep, you've successfully decreased.

Ⓐ

Journaling

I like these journal spaces because…

Twisted Cord

A length of yarn, twisted and tied to stay that way, makes a great purse handle. Want to see for yourself? Gather several pieces of yarn, all the same length. Grab a friend to help, or use a doorknob. (Not that you could ever substitute a doorknob for a friend!)

1. Lay all the strands of yarn together. Using all the strands at once, tie one big knot at each end.

2. Hold a knot in each hand and pull the yarn tight. (If the strands are too long for your arms, have a friend hold one end, or hang that end over a doorknob.) Rotate one knot (right or left, it doesn't matter) again and again until the yarn is tightly twisted into a cord. Ⓐ (Stop before the cord starts to pull against itself and kink. If the cord starts to kink, unwind a little until the kink disappears.)

3. Still keeping the cord tight, have your friend grab the center of the cord with one finger. (Or catch the center of the cord on the underside of a doorknob.) Fold the knots together and hold them in one hand as your friend pulls on the center of the cord to keep it tight. Ⓑ

4. Take over holding the center and slowly release the tension. The cord will begin twisting on itself. Use your finger to turn the center of the cord in the direction of the twist to help it twist up completely. Ⓒ

5. Undo any kinks in the cord, and then knot the knotted ends of the cord together.

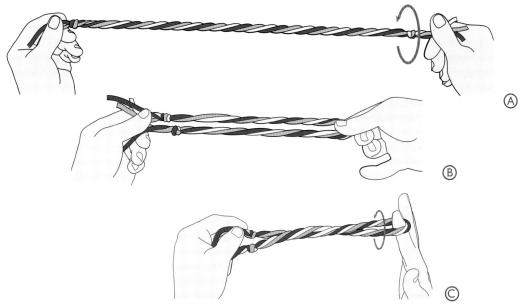

Ⓐ

Ⓑ

Ⓒ

Triangle Kerchief

This stretchy kerchief will handle all your hair, and you see how good it looks.

Size

The triangle measures inches (41 cm) from bas to point

What You Need

- 80 yards (73 m) bulky weight yarn (I used C linette Tagiliatelli #12.
- Knitting needles size US #11 (8 mm)
- Scissors
- Tape measure
- Tapestry needle

Gauge

3 stitches (sts) = 1 inch (2.5 cm) in garter stitch (knit every stitch in eac row)

Skills You'll Use

- Cast On (page 12)
- Knit Stitch (page 14)
- Knit Two Together (page 38)
- Bind Off (page 15)
- Weave In Ends (page 16)

What You Do

1.   Begin by knitting the kerchief ties. Cast on (CO) 150 stitches (sts).

2.   Knit (K) 4 rows.

3.   Time to finish one of the kerchief ties. Bind off (BO) 50 sts (you should have 99 sts remaining on the left needle and 1 st on the right needle for a total of 100 sts). Finish knitting the row.

4.   To finish the other kerchief tie, BO 50 sts (you should have 49 sts remaining on the left needle and 1 st left on the right needle for a total of 50 sts). Finish knitting the row.

5.   To shape the triangular section of the kerchief, K 1 st, knit two together (k2tog), K to the end of the row.

6.   Repeat step 5 until 3 sts remain.

7.   BO all sts.

8.   Weave in the ends. Your kerchief is ready.

Journaling

So far I've done most of my knitting

◯ with friends   ◯ with family   ◯ alone   ◯ other

◯ in the car   ◯ on the bus   ◯ at home   ◯ somewhere else, because…

Envy-Me Envelope Purse

You deserve a purse that's as fun to knit as it is to carry. Just get used to saying, "Oh, you can't buy it anywhere—I made it."

Size

7 inches (18 cm) wide and
5 inches tall (13 cm)

What You Need

• 110 yards (100.5 m) bulky
  weight yarn (I used Classic
  Elite Paintbox #6897.)
• Knitting needles size
  US #8 (5 mm)
• Scissors
• Tape measure
• Tapestry needle
• Button
• 3 inches (8 cm) ribbon

Gauge

4 stitches (sts) = 1 inch (2.5
cm) in garter stitch (knit
every stitch of each row)

Skills You'll Use

• Cast On (page 12)
• Knit Stitch (page 14)
• Knit Two Together (page 38)
• Bind Off (page 15)
• Whip Stitch (page 22)
• Twisted Cord (page 39)

What You Do

Note: In this project, the stitches will seem small and a little tight.
They are supposed to be snug. This helps keep anything from falling
through your purse.

1. You're starting at the top inside edge of the
   purse and will knit the front, the back, and
   the flap. Cast on (CO) 30 stitches (sts).

2. Knit (K) all rows until the piece measures
   10 inches (26 cm).

3. Time to shape the purse's flap. K 1 stitch
   (st), knit two together (k2tog), K each of
   the remaining sts to end of row.

4. Repeat the last row until 3 sts remain on
   the needle.

5. Bind off (BO) remaining sts.

6. To finish your bag, fold it so that the cast-
   on edge lies on top of the last row—before
   the flap shaping. Whip stitch the sides together.
   Turn the bag "right side" out, so that the whip
   stitches are inside the bag.

7. To make a strap, cut four pieces of yarn,
   each 4 yards (3.7 m) long, and make a
   twisted cord.

(continued on next page)

8.   Sew the strap inside the purse edges
          with yarn and your tapestry needle.
      How easy was that?

9.   Sew the button where you'd like it.

10.   Sew a piece of ribbon on the tip of the
          purse flap—on the inside. Wind the
      ribbon around the button to close the purse.
      (Cut the ribbon to length as needed.)

*This purse was made from Plymouth
Eros #2010 yarn and Crystal Palace
Fling #9491 yarn for the flap, and
Cascade Yarns' Cascade 220 in color
7802 for the body.*

Tubes, Tassels, Pom-poms & More

Chapter 3

Write a caption?

Picture Place

Swatch
Pocket

Tubes, Tassels, Pom-Poms & More

If you're ready to knit a hat, a neck warmer, plus the longest scarf you've ever seen, this is the chapter for you. You'll use a technique called **knitting in the round**. I'll show you how, and you can give it a try when you make the projects you see on this page. The project patterns begin on page 52.

Circular Knitting

Knitting in the round is also called **circular knitting**—or **joining in the round**. Try it with a pair of circular needles. You cast on stitches, slide them to the other end of the needles, and create the first stitch of the next round in the first cast-on loop. (When knitting in rows, the first stitch of the next row is created in the last cast-on loop). Creating the first stitch in the first cast-on loop joins the work into a **round**.

To practice this skill, grab a smooth, bulky weight yarn, (see page 7 for the Yarn Weights Chart) and a 16-inch circular needle, size US #11 (8 mm). (Select a needle size that is recommended on the yarn label. If there is no label, use a needle that is a little larger than the thickness of your yarn). You'll also need a table or flat surface and a stitch marker. (See page 31.) Make sure you have at least 20 yards (18 m) of yarn.

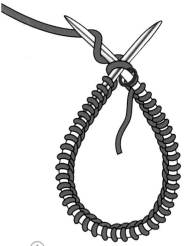

1.   Use your circular needle to cast on 60 stitches.

2.   Place your needle (with tips pointing together) on a table. Look at your cast on stitches. Slide the last stitch you cast on up near the tip of the right needle. Make sure all the bumps from your cast on lay to the inside of the circle as your needle lies on the table. Scoot the first cast-on loop to the tip of the left needle. Make one final check that all the bumps lie to the inside. Now you are ready to make the join.

3.   Place a stitch marker on the right needle and pick up the right needle with your right hand. Ⓐ Hold the last cast-on loop and stitch marker near the tip with your pointer finger. Pick up the left needle with your left hand and hold the first cast-on loop near the tip. Pick up the needles and create a knit stitch.

4.   You have just joined your knitting in the round. Knit all the way around until you get back to the stitch marker. What you just created is called a round, not a row. Way to go!

Ⓐ

Going Round with Double Pointed Needles

You can also use double pointed needles to knit in the round. Double pointed needles are best for making circles and smaller tubes, like the top of a hat. (Your circular needles might be too long and get in the way of your work.) I like to use three double pointed needles to hold the stitches, and one more double pointed needle to create the new stitches. As you use them, the three needles form a triangle, with the tips of the needles overlapping. (Sometimes knitters use four needles to hold the stitches.)

Ready to try it? You'll need a piece of knitting in the round that is still on a circular needle, the same yarn used on the circular needle, and four double pointed needles the same size as the circular needle.

1. First, figure out how many stitches to put on each double pointed needle. Count the total number of stitches on the circular needle and divide by 3. If your number doesn't evenly divide, put the extra stitches on the third needle. The exact stitch count isn't critical; it just helps to spread out the stitches.

2. Now begin transferring the stitches from the circular needle to the first double pointed needle. Hold a double pointed needle in your right hand and the circular needle in your left hand; the yarn should be coming from the end of the circular needle that you're not holding. (You might feel like you have three thumbs, but you can do this.)

3. Put the tip of the double pointed needle into the first stitch on the left needle.

4. Wrap the double pointed needle in the usual way and complete the stitch. You might have to give a little tug to tighten up the slack between the loose end of the circular needle and the double pointed needle. Continue working stitches this way until you have worked the number of stitches calculated in step 1.

(continued on next page)

5.   Release the double pointed needle; be careful that the stitches do not slide off this needle as you continue working. Pick up your next double pointed needle with your right hand.

6.   Repeat steps 3 through 5 to transfer stitches to the second double pointed needle.

7.   Repeat steps 3 through 5 to transfer stitches to the third double pointed needle. Remember that you may need to transfer a few more stitches onto the third needle.

8.   Now all of your stitches are on the double pointed needles and the circular needle is empty. The three double pointed needles should be overlapping slightly and forming a triangular shape. The yarn should be coming from the third double pointed needle.

9.   You will now begin knitting using only the double pointed needles. Pick up your fourth double pointed needle with your right hand and hold the first double pointed needle in your left hand to begin your next round. Ⓐ

Ⓐ

10.   Put the tip of the fourth double pointed needle into the first stitch on the first double pointed needle, wrap the yarn and complete the stitch as usual. Continue working stitches until the first double pointed needle is empty.

11.   Repeat step 10 using the first double pointed needle to work all the stitches on the second double pointed needle. Then use the second double pointed needle to work all the stitches on the third double pointed needle. You have now completed a round using double pointed needles.

12.   Continue working in this manner until the tube is the desired length. Nice work!

Pattern Repeats

Sometimes a pattern wants you to do the same thing over and over in the same row. In order to keep the pattern short, the patterns are sometimes written in an abbreviated way:

*Knit two together (k2tog); repeat from * to end of the round.

You will do what it says and then you will repeat what is between the asterisks (*). So for this direction, you would knit two stitches together, and then the repeat tells you to knit two stitches together again and again and again, etc., until you get to the end of the round.

Tassel

A **tassel** looks a lot like fringe, only it dangles from a strand of yarn instead of hanging off the edges of a project. It's an easy, fun finishing touch. To make one, gather a piece of heavy cardboard or a small book, yarn, a tapestry needle, and scissors.

1.   Cut a piece of heavy cardboard close to the length you want your tassel to be.

2.   Cut two lengths of yarn about 12 inches (30 cm) long. One piece is your tying yarn, the other is your wrapping yarn.

3.   Wrap one length of yarn around the cardboard. The more wraps you have, the fatter your tassel will be.

4.   Thread a tapestry needle with the tying yarn. Insert the needle under the yarn wraps near one edge of the cardboard and tie a knot around the wraps with this yarn. This is the top of the tassel. The tying yarn will be used to attach your tassel to your project. Ⓐ

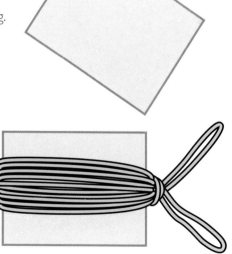

(continued on next page)

Ⓐ

49

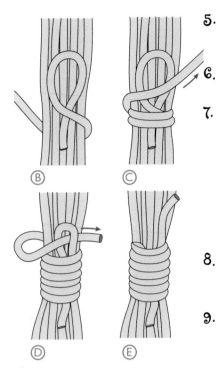

(B)

(C)

(D)

(E)

5. Cut the yarn wraps at the end opposite to the tie you just made. Remove the cardboard.

6. Hold the tassel so the cut ends hang downward.

7. Place the end of the wrapping yarn near the cut ends of the tassel. Make a loop in the wrapping yarn near the top of the tassel. Beginning about 1½ inches (4 cm) from the top of the tassel, wrap the yarn around the tassel and over the looped end. (B) Continue wrapping toward the top of the yarn. Each wrap should be right next to the one you just did. Continue to wrap for about ½ inch (1 cm). (C)

8. Put the end of the wrapping yarn through its loop near the top of the tassel. (D)

9. Slowly pull the other end of the wrapping yarn that is near the cut ends of the tassel. (E) This will pull the wrapping yarn under the wraps so it looks nice. If the tails stick out, you can trim them. (I learned this fancy wrapping technique in Girl Scouts.)

10. Use the scissors to trim the ends so they are even. (F) Attach the tassel to the project using the tying yarn. Now make as many tassels as you like.

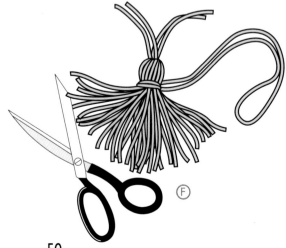

(F)

Pom-Poms

Pom-poms are too fun to be just for cheerleaders. Whether you make them small or jumbo sized, pom-poms stand out and get your knits noticed. To practice making a pom-pom, all you need is a ball of yarn and scissors. It helps to have a friend nearby.

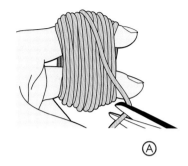

1. Wrap yarn around the the first and second fingers on your nondominant hand. More wraps will make a fuller pom-pom. Go crazy. Then cut the yarn from the ball. Ⓐ

Ⓐ

2. Wrap the tying yarn (the loose end) around the center of all the loops and tie a tight knot. (You could ask your friend to do this step.) Ⓑ

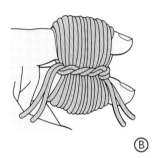

3. Slide your fingers out of the yarn. Cut both ends of all the yarn loops. Then use the scissors to give your pom-pom a haircut to smooth it out and shape it. How does it look? Ⓒ

Ⓑ

4. Attach the pom-pom to any project by tying it with a length of yarn. Make sure your knot is on the inside of the project.

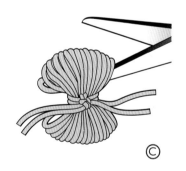

Ⓒ

Swatch Watch

Who says you can only save swatches in the pockets in this book? Tuck your practice tassels and pom-poms in there, too!

Around-Your-Neck Scarf

What's warmer and cooler than a turtleneck?
A colorful tube scarf that you knit yourself.

Size
6 inches (15 cm) tall and 2▮
inches (53 cm) around

What You Need
- 100 yards (120 m) bulky
  weight yarn (I used Norc▮
  Iro #56.)
- 16-inch (40-cm) circular
  knitting needle size
  US #11 (8 mm)
- Scissors
- Stitch marker
- Tape measure
- Tapestry needle

Gauge
3 stitches (sts) = 1 inch
(2.5 cm)

Skills You'll Use
- Cast On (page 12)
- Joining in the Round
  (page 46)
- Knit Stitch (page 14)
- Bind Off (page 15)
- Weave In Ends (page 16)

This scarf is made with Plymouth Yarn Mira Mira #2744 and Brazilia Fantasy Color #386 yarn. ►

What You Do

1. Cast on (CO) 65 stitches (sts) to create the width of your scarf. You're knitting a tube, so you need to carefully spread out your sts on the needle and check that they are all going in the same direction.

2. The needle connected to the yarn ball should be in your right hand and the other needle in the left. Place marker (PM) on the tip of the right needle.

3. Begin knitting the first stitch (st) on the left needle. When you knit all the way around to the marker, you've completed one round. Keep going.

4. Knit (K) all rounds until your piece measures 6 inches (15 cm).

5. Bind off (BO) all sts.

6. Weave in all ends. You're finished! How long can you make yourself wait before you try it on?

Journaling

My friends who knit are…

....

My friends who might like to learn to knit are…

....

How could I show them how fun knitting is?

....

Follow the
Rainbow Scarf

Finally, a super long, super colorful scarf to go with anything you wear. Okay, maybe not plaid!

Size
8 inches (21 cm) wide and 72 inches long (138 cm)

What You Need
- 6 different colors worsted weight yarn, 130 yards (119 m) of each (I used Cascade Pastaza #049 [red], #076 [orange], #068 [blue], #079 [green], #054 [purple], Rio de la Plata #A39 [gold fusion].)
- 16-inch (40-cm) circular knitting needles size US #9 (5.5 mm)
- Crochet hook size J
- Scissors
- Stitch marker
- Tape measure
- Tapestry needle

Gauge
4 stitches (sts) = 1 inch (2.5 cm) in stockinette stitch (when working in the round, this means knit all the stitches)

Skills You'll Use
- Cast On (page 12)
- Joining in the Round (page 46)
- Knit Stitch (page 14)
- Joining Yarn (page 20)
- Bind Off (page 15)
- Fringe (page 21)

I knitted a different number of rows for each color on this scarf. Each time I started a new color, I picked a different yarn. This is a great way to use your leftover pieces of yarn.

Here's How

1. With your main color and your circular needle, cast on (CO) 60 stitches (sts). Place marker (PM). Join in the round, being careful not to twist the stitches over the needle as you join.

2. Knit (K) 10 rounds of your first color (red).

3. Change to your second color (orange) and K 10 rounds. Since you are making a tube scarf, the inside of the tube will never be seen. When you change colors, feel free to simply knot these colors together and leave the tails loose inside.

4. Time to create a rainbow of stripes!

   Step 1: Change to your third color (yellow). K 10 rounds.

   Step 2: Change to your fourth color (green). K 10 rounds. (Are you noticing a pattern?)

   Step 3: Change to your fifth color (blue). K 10 rounds.

   Step 4: Now change to your sixth color (purple). K 10 rounds.

5. Repeat the pattern from step 4 until your scarf measures 72 inches (183 cm) or your desired length. End with your sixth color (purple).

6. Bind off (BO) all sts.

7. Finish your scarf by adding fringe. Cut 24 pieces from each yarn color. Make each fringe with 6 pieces of one color. Put 12 fringes on each end of your scarf, pulling the yarn through both layers of the scarf. When you fringe the second end, lay the scarf flat to make sure the tube is straight before you attach the fringe. Whew! You're done.

Happy Hat

Yes, you'll look tasselrific in this hat. Just don't be pom-pompous about it.

Size
Fits most youth

What You Need
- 125 yards (114 m) bulky weight yarn for the main color (I used Brown Sheep Lamb's Pride Bulky #M130.)
- 80 yards (73 m) bulky weight yarn for the contrast color (I used Brown Sheep Lamb's Pride Bulky #M120.)
- 16-inch (40-cm) circular knitting needle size US #11 (8 mm)
- Four double pointed knitting needles size US #11 (8 mm)
- Scissors
- Stitch marker
- Tape measure
- Tapestry needle
- Heavy cardboard

Gauge
3 stitches (sts) = 1 inch (2.5 cm) and 5 rows = 1 inch (2.5 cm)

Skills You'll Use
- Cast On (page 12)
- Joining in the Round (page 46)
- Knit Stitch (page 14)
- Joining Yarn (page 20)
- Knitting with Double Pointed Needles (page 47)
- Knit Two Together (page 38)
- Bind Off (page 15)
- Tassel (page 49)
- Weave In Ends (page 16)

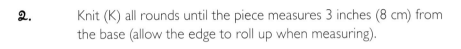

What You Do

1. Using your main color and the circular needle, cast on (CO) 60 stitches (sts). Place marker (PM) and join in the round, being careful not to twist stitches. This is the hat's bottom edge.

2. Knit (K) all rounds until the piece measures 3 inches (8 cm) from the base (allow the edge to roll up when measuring).

3. Change to contrasting color and K 4 rounds to create the stripe.

4. Change back to main color and K until piece measure 6½ inches (17 cm) from the base (allow the edge to roll up when measuring).

5. K one more round and change to your double pointed needles. Then put 20 sts on each double pointed needle.

6. Time to shape the top of your hat. Decrease your knitting as follows:

☐ **Round 1:** *Knit two together (k2tog); repeat from * to end of the round. (30 sts, 10 on each needle)

☐ **Round 2:** K all sts.

☐ **Round 3:** *K2tog; repeat from * to end of the round. (15 sts, 5 on each needle)

☐ **Round 4:** K all sts

☐ **Round 5:** *K2tog; repeat from * ending with K 1 stitch (st). Note: At the end of the first needle, move the last stitch to the second needle so you can knit it together with the next stitch. Work across needle. At the end of the third needle, you will have 1 st left. K this st. (8 sts)

(continued on next page)

7. Ready to start finishing? Cut yarn, leaving a 12-inch (31 cm) length. Thread the yarn on your tapestry needle. Insert the needle into each of the remaining stitches and remove the knitting needle. Pull tight to draw the stitches together. Insert the needle through the center of the top to the inside. Weave in the end on the inside of the hat.

8. Make a tassel.

9. Make a braid that will be used to attach the tassel. Cut three pieces of yarn, each 10 inches (26 cm) long. Hold all three pieces together and tie a knot about 3 inches (8 cm) from one end. Braid the strands together for 4 inches (10 cm). Tie a knot at the end of the braid.

10. Attach the braid to the tassel by putting two pieces of the end of the braid through the fold of the tassel. Use the third piece to make a knot with the other 2.

11. Now attach the other end of the braid to the top of the hat. Thread one of the tails on your tapestry needle and poke it into a stitch next to the center hole. Thread another tail on your tapestry needle and poke it into the other side of the center hole. (This will help avoid a lopsided tassel.) Repeat with the third tail. Tie them together on the inside and weave in your ends. You made a hat!

Journaling

Fill in the chart with your favorite people, their birthdays, and things you can knit for them as gifts.

example: *Mom*	*April 10*	*bookmark*

Ruffles & Diagonals

What will you paste here?

Picture Place

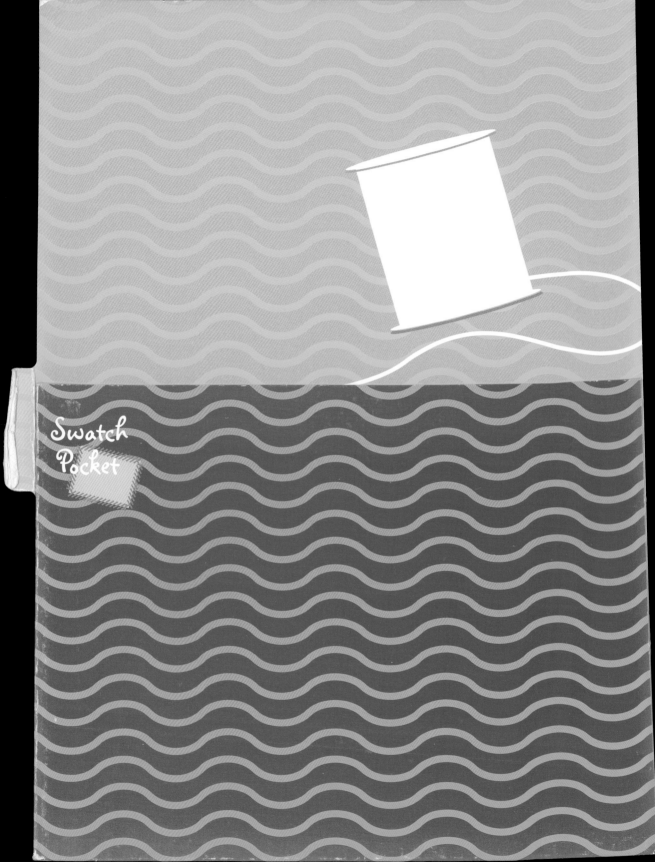

Swatch
Pocket

Ruffles & Diagonals

Ruffles on the edge of a piece are one of my favorite details to add. Sometimes it makes all the difference in the world. Knitting in a diagonal—so it looks as if the knitting is going diagonally instead of straight across—is a close second. Give these techniques a try when you make the projects you see on this page. The project patterns begin on page 61.

Knit in the Front and Back of the Stitch

You create ruffles by making a dramatic change in the number of stitches in a row. One way to do this is by **knitting in the front and the back of a stitch**, which is an **increasing** technique. Grab a piece of knitting still on the needles, with the yarn still attached, to practice this skill.

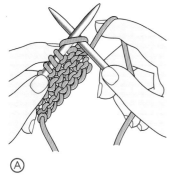

(A)

1.   Insert the tip of the right needle into the stitch on the left needle as if to knit. Knit the stitch, but do not remove it from the left needle. (A)

(B)

2.   Insert the tip of your right needle into the back loop of the same stitch on the left needle. Wrap the yarn around the right needle as usual and pull the yarn through the loop. (B) (C)

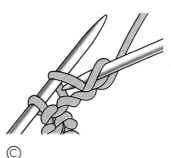

(C)

3.   Finish the knit stitch by taking the stitch off the left hand needle. Then knit the remaining stitches in the usual way.

4.   Count the stitches on your row. Notice you have one more stitch than before. That's exactly what you want. (D) (

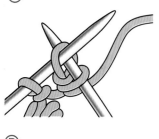

(D)

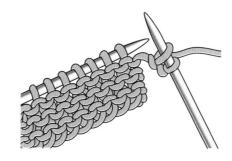

(E)

Look-At-Me Purse

Are you the kind of girl who can handle being the center of attention? This tall purse with an eye-catching design is just for you.

Size

5 inches (13 cm) wide and 8 inches (21 cm) tall

What You Need

- 124 yards (113 m) bulky weight yarn (I used Reynolds Smile #103.)
- Knitting needles size US #10 (6 mm)
- 2-inch (5-cm) button
- Scissors
- Tape measure
- Tapestry needle

Gauge

3 stitches (sts) = 1 inch (2.5 cm)

Skills You'll Use

- Cast On (page 12)
- Knit Stitch (page 14)
- Knit in Front & Back of Stitch (page 60)
- Knit Two Together (page 38)
- Bind Off (page 15)
- Twisted Cord (page 39)
- Whip Stitch (page 22)
- Weave In Ends (page 16)

What You Do

1. Start knitting at a corner of the top opening of the purse. Cast on (CO) 2 stitches (sts).

2. Your work increases as follows:

☐ **Row 1:** Knit (K) all sts

☐ **Row 2:** Knit in the front and back of the stitch (kf&b), kf&b (4 sts)

☐ **Row 3:** K all sts

☐ **Row 4:** Kf&b, k 2, kf&b (6 sts)

☐ **Row 5:** K all sts

☐ **Row 6:** Kf&b, k 4, kf&b (8 sts)

☐ **Row 7:** K all sts

☐ **Row 8:** Kf&b, k 6, kf&b (10 sts)

☐ **Row 9:** K all sts

☐ **Row 10:** Kf&b, k 8, kf&b (12 sts)

☐ **Row 11:** K all sts

☐ **Row 12:** Kf&b, k 10, kf&b (14 sts)

☐ **Row 13:** K all sts

☐ **Row 14:** Kf&b, k 12, kf&b (16 sts)

☐ **Row 15:** K all sts

☐ **Row 16:** Kf&b, k 14, kf&b (18 sts)

☐ **Row 17:** K all sts

☐ **Row 18:** Kf&b, k 16, kf&b (20 sts)

☐ **Row 19:** K all sts

☐ **Row 20:** Kf&b, k 18, kf&b (22 sts)

☐ **Row 21:** K all sts

☐ **Row 22:** Kf&b, k 20, kf&b (24 sts)

☐ **Row 23:** K all sts

☐ **Row 24:** Kf&b, k 22, kf&b (26 sts)

☐ **Row 25:** K all sts

Note: You now have all the stitches you need. In order to keep the stitch count constant and continue the bias (a diagonal), you have to increase and decrease on the same row.

☐ **Row 26:** Knit two together, k 23, kf&b

☐ **Row 27:** K all sts

3. Repeat the last 2 rows until your piece measures 20 inches (51 cm) tall when measured on the shortest side.

Note: Your piece will have a straight bottom where you started and a diagonal edge where your needle is. Make certain to measure the shorter side.

4. Bind off (BO) all sts.

5. To begin finishing your purse, fold the piece so the straight bottom meets just below the lowest side of the bind-off edge. The front length of the purse is 8 inches (21 cm). Whip stitch both side seams.

6. Cut 10 pieces of yarn, each 3½ yards (3 m) long, and make the twisted cord. Sew the ends of the twisted cord strap to the inside corners of the purse to form the handle.

7. Sew the button onto the lower left corner. Weave in all ends.

8. Sew a piece of ribbon on the tip of the purse flap. Wind the ribbon around the button to close the purse.

Music & Movies Tote

This bag is just the right size for carrying CDs and DVDs. A simple ribbon and button combo holds everything in place.

Size

6 inches (15 cm) wide and 6 inches (15 cm) tall

What You Need

- 100 yards (91.5 m) bulky weight yarn (I used Noro Iro #18.)
- Knitting needles size US #10 (6 mm)
- 6 inches (15 cm) of ribbon
- 1-inch (25-mm) button (I used a Tagua Slice button from One World Button Supply Company)
- Scissors
- Tape measure
- Tapestry needle

Gauge

3 stitches (sts) = 1 inch (2.5 cm) in garter stitch (knit every stitch in each row)

Skills You'll Use

- Cast On (page 12)
- Knit Stitch (page 14)
- Knit Two Together (page 38)
- Knit in Front & Back of Stitch (page 60)
- Weave In Ends (page 16)
- Whip Stitch (page 22)
- Bind Off (page 15)

What You Do

1. Begin knitting the width of your project. Cast on (CO) 30 stitches (sts).

2. Knit (K) 1 row.

3. Knit two together (k2tog). K to last stitch (st). Knit in the front and back of the stitch (Kf&b) in last st.

4. Repeat last 2 rows until piece measures 13 inches (33 cm).

5. Bind off (BO) all sts.

6. To begin finishing your tote, weave in all ends.

7. Whip stitch the cast-on edge to the bind-off edge, creating a diagonal seam. Sew one straight edge of the square closed to create a bottom for the tote.

8. To make handles, CO 5 sts. K all rows until the piece measures 48 inches (122 cm). BO all sts.

9. Use the tails to sew the handles to the top of the bag. Sew one end to the inside of the purse back and one to the inside of the purse front.

10. Fold the ribbon in half and tie a knot about 1 inch (2.5 cm) from the fold to create a loop for the button. Insert the tails (one at a time in different places) from the outside of the purse to the inside of the purse and tie them in a knot.

11. Sew the button to the front side so the knotted ribbon will fit around it. You're done.

Journaling

My Favorite Movie

· ·

My Favorite Song

· ·

Ruffle Scarf

Do you think the ruffles make this scarf look sweet or sophisticated? It's a good thing you can pull off either look.

Size

2 inches (5 cm) wide and 40 inches (102 cm) long

What You Need

- Worsted weight yarn 100 yards (120 m) (I used Artyarns Supermerino 8 #107.)
- Knitting needles size US #9 (5.5 mm)
- Scissors
- Tape measure
- Tapestry needle

Gauge

3 stitches (sts) = 1 inch (2.5 cm) in garter stitch (knit every stitch of each row)

Skills You'll Use

- Cast On (page 12)
- Knit Stitch (page 14)
- Knit Two Together (page 38)
- Knit in Front & Back of Stitch (page 60)
- Bind Off (page 15)
- Weave In Ends (page 16)

I've made fringe, I've made ruffles… If I had to choose a favorite add-on detail, I'd pick…

....

....

....

....

....

What You Do

1.   Cast on (CO) 40 stitches (sts).

2.   Work decreases as follows:

☐ **Row 1:** Knit (K) all sts

☐ **Row 2:** *Knit two together (k2tog); repeat from * across the row (20 sts)

☐ **Row 3:** K all sts

☐ **Row 4:** K all sts

☐ **Row 5:** K all sts

☐ **Row 6:** *K2tog; repeat from * across the row (10 sts)

3.   K all rows until the piece is 40 inches (102 cm) long or as long as you'd like it to be.

4.   Work increases as follows:

☐ **Row 1:** *Knit in the front and back of the stitch (Kf&b); repeat from* across the row (20 sts)

☐ **Row 2:** K all sts

☐ **Row 3:** K all sts

☐ **Row 4:** K all sts

☐ **Row 5:** *Kf&b; repeat from* across the row (40 sts)

☐ **Row 6:** K all sts

5.   Bind off (BO) all sts.

6.   To finish your scarf, weave in all ends. How's it look?

Textures & Sizing

Easy Breezy Tank Top

Cozy Cashmere Cuffs

Bright & Beautiful Backpack

Funky Flip-Flops

Tape a photo here.

Make sure to include
pictures of your friends!

Picture
Place

Chapter 5

Textures & Sizing

Did you know that knitted clothes and accessories can be smooth on one side and bumpy on the other? There's also more than one way to sew knitted pieces together.

Are you wondering how to make sure the clothes you make will fit? This chapter tackles those questions, so you can make the projects you see on this page. The project patterns begin on page 74.

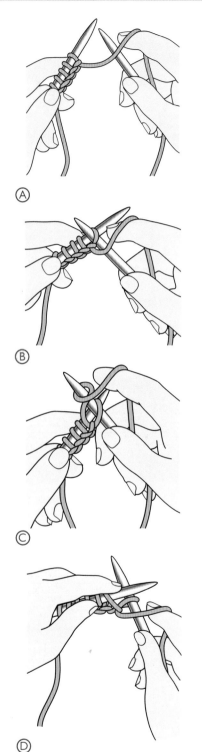

(A)

(B)

(C)

(D)

Purl Stitch

Did you know there is a second knitting stitch? It's called a **purl stitch**. All **stitch patterns** are a combination or variation of **knitting** and **purling**. One way to create texture (a smooth side and an opposite bumpy side on your knits) is to combine rows of knit stitches and rows of purl stitches.

To practice purl stitching, grab a smooth, worsted weight yarn and a pair of needles. (See page 7 for the Yarn Weights Chart.) Select a needle size recommended on the yarn label. If there is no label, use a needle a little larger than the thickness of your yarn. Make sure you have at least 20 yards (18 m) of yarn.

1. Cast on about 15 stitches. Hold the needle with the cast-on stitches in your left hand. (A)

2. Place the tip of the right needle on the right side of the first stitch on the left needle. Push the tip of the right needle from right to left under the front strand of the stitch. The needles will form an X. The right needle should be on the top of the X. (B)

3. Grab the working yarn with your right hand and wrap the yarn around the top needle by bringing the yarn under the needle, from right to left, and then back over the needle, from left to right. Allow the yarn to slip into the center of the X. (C)

4. Move the tip of the right needle down, away from you, and out the back of the stitch. As you move the right needle, use the tip to draw the yarn wrap through the stitch. This movement is opposite to how you put your needle into the stitch. There should be a loop of yarn on your needle when it comes out of the stitch. (D)

5. Slide the right needle to the right until the first stitch on the left needle moves completely off the needle. You've just created your first purl stitch. Ⓔ

6. Repeat steps 2 through 5 with each stitch on your needle. When you finish your row, all the stitches will be on the right needle and your left needle will be empty. Trade hands to begin the new row.

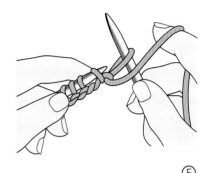

Ⓔ

Journaling

My favorite yarn is

....

because

....

My favorite knitting technique is

....

because

....

Stockinette Stitch

The **stockinette stitch** is another technique that creates a smooth side and a bumpy side. A stockinette stitch is a combination of knit and purl stitches; it's sometimes called a stitch pattern. It's easy to do. Want to give it a try?

You'll need smooth, worsted weight yarn and a pair of needles. (See page 7 for the Yarn Weights Chart.) Select a needle size recommended on the yarn label. If there is no label, use a needle a little larger than the thickness of your yarn. Make sure you have at least 20 yards (18 m) of yarn.

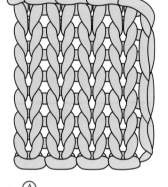

(A)

1. Cast on about 15 stitches.

2. Knit one row.

3. Purl one row.

4. Repeat steps 2 and 3 until the piece is the desired size. Notice that one side is smooth with V-shaped stitches and the other side is bumpy and looks similar to the garter stitch pattern. You did it! (A)

An easy way to know whether you need to knit or purl the row is to look at the knitting. If you are looking at the smooth side, you will knit the row. If you are looking at the bumpy side, you will purl the row.

 Swatch Watch

Was this your first time knitting a stockinette stitch? Why not save your practice piece? Turn to the nearest Swatch Watch pocket. Stow it there!

Mattress Stitch

There are lots of ways to sew your knitting together. I like the way a **mattress stitch** looks, so I use it often. Sewing always creates a **seam**, which is the line where the pieces come together. If you use a mattress stitch to connect two pieces of stockinette stitch, the seam is almost invisible. To practice this technique, gather two pieces of knitting that you wish to sew together, yarn that matches the yarn in your project (about 2 inches [5 cm] of yarn per inch of seam), a tapestry needle and scissors. Make sure that you have enough matching yarn to sew all the seams you want to make.

Before you begin, examine the edges of your knitting. Be sure to stitch the pieces together along the edges, not the cast-on or bind-off ends. Also, remember to stitch in the spaces between the last two stitches of the rows.

1. Lay both pieces out flat so you are looking at the outside of the fabric. In stockinette stitch, the outside is the smooth side.

2. Thread your tapestry needle with your yarn. Push the needle from the back to the front in the corner of the piece on the left side, leaving a 6 to 8 inch (15 to 20 cm) tail. Then go to the piece on the right side and come up in that corner the same way. You have just created a lock so your yarn won't pull out too easily as you stitch.

Ⓐ

3. Insert the needle, from front to back in the spot on the left piece where you see the yarn coming out from your last stitch. Move the tip of the needle so it goes under two horizontal bars located between the last two stitches. Push the needle to the front of the work and pull it through. Leave the sewing loose; you will tighten it later. Ⓐ

4. Insert the needle from front to back in the spot on the right piece where the yarn is coming out. Move the needle under two horizontal bars and push it to the front of the work and pull it through.

(continued on next page)

5. Repeat steps 3 and 4 until the seam is complete.

6. Pull the loose strands tight, one at a time. Weave in the ends. You've completed a mattress stitch.

Do a few inches of seaming before you pull the yarn tight. This way, you can see where you need to put your needle.

When you get close to the end of your seam, check to see if both sides still look about the same length. If one side looks longer, you can fudge the seam to ease the longer piece in by going under three bars on the longer side.

Get a Good Fit

The sizes you see in clothing patterns are different from your regular shirt or pants sizes. To find your size, all you need is a tape measure. (Use the soft kind that easily wraps around your body, not the metal kind that you use for woodworking projects.)

If you're making a top, measure your chest at its fullest part. (For the most accurate result, measure while you're wearing the kind of undergarments you'd wear under the top.) Chest: _____ Depending on how you want your clothes to fit, add 2 to 6 inches (5 to 15 cm) to your body measurement. (Two inches gives you a snug fit. Six inches gives you a loose, comfortable fit.) Write the total (your size) here _____ .

For a skirt, measure your hips at their fullest part. Hips:_____ Skirts require more ease (room between the fabric and the body) than tops—so you can walk and bend in them. I've included the ease in my Swish Sway Swing skirt pattern on page 99. So use your actual hip measurement to find your size in that pattern.

As long as you already have the tape measure out, why not fill in the chart on the next page? You can record measurements for you and your friends.

Since I don't know what sizes you wear, my clothes patterns tell you how to make several different sizes. A description might read: "Fits sizes 28 (30, 32, 34, 36) inches [71 (76, 81, 86.5, 91.5) cm]." To keep track of what you're making, just circle your size. In the instructions, I put the number of stitches in parentheses to match what's listed in the size section. It looks like this:

Cast on (CO) 12 (16, 20, 24, 28).

If you're making something for a size 28, follow the instructions for the number before the parentheses. So, you'll cast on 12 stitches. If you're knitting for a size 32, cast on 20 stitches. Make sense? To make it even easier, go through each project pattern's instructions before you start knitting clothes for yourself. Circle all numbers that go with the size you are making.

Actual Measurement	Finished Garment Measurement		
	For a Snug Fit	For a Close Fit	For a Loose Fit
Name			
Chest (inches or cm) _____	+2 inches (5 cm) = _____	+4 inches (10 cm) = _____	+6 inches (15 cm) = _____
Hip (inches or cm) _____	+10 inches (25 cm) = _____	+12 inches (30 cm) = _____	+14 inches (35 cm) = _____
Name			
Chest (inches or cm) _____	+2 inches (5 cm) = _____	+4 inches (10 cm) = _____	+6 inches (15 cm) = _____
Hip (inches or cm) _____	+10 inches (25 cm) = _____	+12 inches (30 cm) = _____	+14 inches (35 cm) = _____
Name			
Chest (inches or cm) _____	+2 inches (5 cm) = _____	+4 inches (10 cm) = _____	+6 inches (15 cm) = _____
Hip (inches or cm) _____	+10 inches (25 cm) = _____	+12 inches (30 cm) = _____	+14 inches (35 cm) = _____

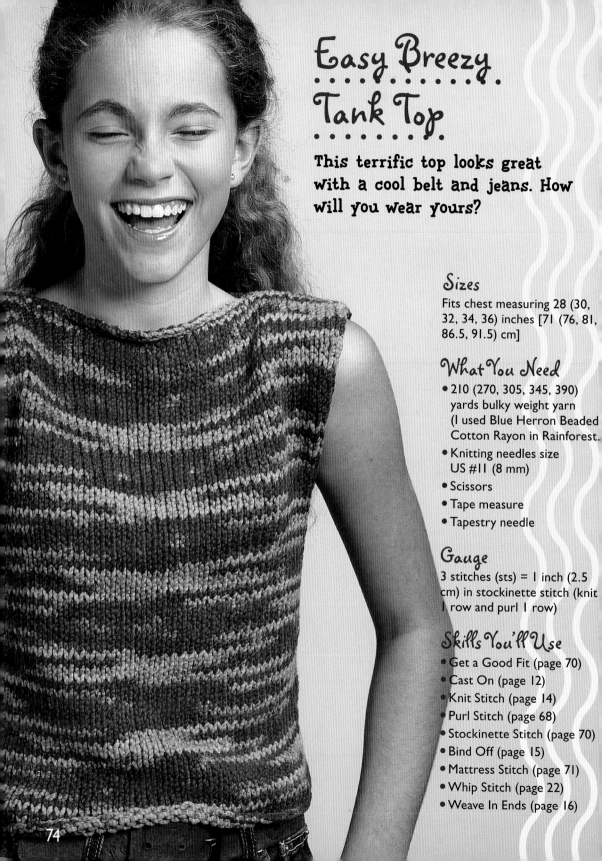

Easy Breezy Tank Top

This terrific top looks great with a cool belt and jeans. How will you wear yours?

Sizes

Fits chest measuring 28 (30, 32, 34, 36) inches [71 (76, 81, 86.5, 91.5) cm]

What You Need

- 210 (270, 305, 345, 390) yards bulky weight yarn (I used Blue Herron Beaded Cotton Rayon in Rainforest.
- Knitting needles size US #11 (8 mm)
- Scissors
- Tape measure
- Tapestry needle

Gauge

3 stitches (sts) = 1 inch (2.5 cm) in stockinette stitch (knit 1 row and purl 1 row)

Skills You'll Use

- Get a Good Fit (page 70)
- Cast On (page 12)
- Knit Stitch (page 14)
- Purl Stitch (page 68)
- Stockinette Stitch (page 70)
- Bind Off (page 15)
- Mattress Stitch (page 71)
- Whip Stitch (page 22)
- Weave In Ends (page 16)

What You Do

1. Before you get started, circle the numbers in these instructions that correspond to the size you want to make. This will keep you from getting confused as you go.

2. You are beginning at the bottom of one side of the tank top and will knit the length. Cast on (CO) 42 (45, 48, 51, 54) stitches (sts). Leave a long tail that can be used for sewing your seams later. About 45 inches (115 cm) ought to be long enough. Roll it up and put a rubber band around it so you don't accidentally knit with it.

3. Work in stockinette stitch (st st) for 15 (16, 17, 18, 19) inches [38 (40.5, 43, 45.5, 48.5) cm] or desired length.

4. Bind off (BO) all sts.

5. Cut your yarn.

6. Repeat steps 2 through 5 to make a second piece, which is the other side of your tank top.

7. Start finishing by sewing the shoulder seams and creating the neck opening. Put the two pieces together with the bumpy side to the inside. Make sure the two bind-off edges are together. Beginning at one corner of the bind-off edge, whip stitch the edges together for 2 inches (5 cm). Weave in the sewing yarn. Beginning at the other bind off corner, make a 2-inch (5-cm) seam from the outer edge toward the center.

8. Now you sew the side seams and create the armholes. Thread a tapestry needle with the long tail you created in the cast on. Begin using the mattress stitch at the cast-on edge, stitch the sides together, stopping 5 to 6 inches (12.5 to 15 cm) from the top edge where you sewed the shoulders. Repeat on the other side. Weave in the sewing yarns.

9. Weave in all other ends. You're done.

Journaling

Up to now I'd only knitted accessories. This is my first top! Next, I'll try…

....

....

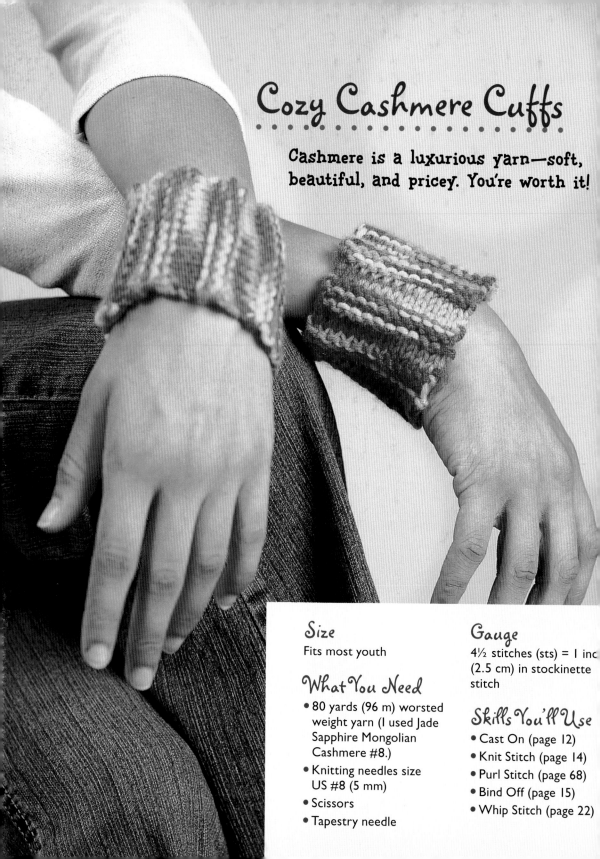

Cozy Cashmere Cuffs

Cashmere is a luxurious yarn—soft, beautiful, and pricey. You're worth it!

Size
Fits most youth

What You Need
- 80 yards (96 m) worsted weight yarn (I used Jade Sapphire Mongolian Cashmere #8.)
- Knitting needles size US #8 (5 mm)
- Scissors
- Tapestry needle

Gauge
4½ stitches (sts) = 1 inc (2.5 cm) in stockinette stitch

Skills You'll Use
- Cast On (page 12)
- Knit Stitch (page 14)
- Purl Stitch (page 68)
- Bind Off (page 15)
- Whip Stitch (page 22)

What You Do

1. Cast on (CO) 12 stitches (sts) to create the width.

2. Now you will start working in a pattern stitch to knit the length of the cuff. The pattern stitch forms ribs that make your cuffs nice and stretchy.

☐ **Row 1:** Purl (P) all sts

☐ **Row 2:** Knit (K) all sts

☐ **Row 3:** P all sts

☐ **Row 4:** P all sts

☐ **Row 5:** K all sts

☐ **Row 6:** P all sts

I used Lobster Pot Cashmere yarn in hydrangea for these cuffs. I added a little fringe with the cashmere Trendsetter Flora #202 and Crystal Palace Fuzz #7223 yarns.

3. Repeat these 6 rows 8 times.

4. Bind off (BO) all sts.

5. To finish your cuffs, whip stitch the bind-off edge to the cast-on edge. Nice job.

Picture Place

Do you have a future as a hand model? Have a friend snap a photo of you in your cuffs. Save it for your portfolio—or scrapbook it in this book!

Bright & Beautiful
Backpack

Tassels and bold colors make this pack fun for school or sleepovers.

Size

12 inches (31 cm) tall,
10 inches (26 cm) wide, and
1 inch (2.5 cm) deep

What You Need

- 300 yards (274.5 m) bulky weight yarn (I used Schaefer Elaine in color Isadora Duncan.)
- 24-inch (60-cm) circular knitting needle, size US #10½ (6.5 mm)
- Scissors
- Stitch marker
- Tape measure
- Tapestry needle

Gauge

3 stitches (sts) = 1 inch (2.5 cm)

Skills You'll Use

- Cast On (page 12)
- Joining in the Round (page 46)
- Knit Stitch (page 14)
- Purl Stitch (page 68)
- Bind Off (page 15)
- Twisted Cord (page 39)
- Whip Stitch (page 22)

What You Do

1. Begin at the bottom of the bag and then knit the length. Cast on (CO) 72 stitches (sts). Place marker (PM) on the right needle. Join in the round, making certain not to twist the sts over the needle.

2. Knit (K) all rounds until your piece measures 12 inches (30.5 cm).

3. Start working in a pattern stitch. The rounds of the pattern stitch form the top edge of the backpack.

☐ **Round 1:** Purl (P) all sts

☐ **Round 2:** K all sts

☐ **Round 3:** P all sts

☐ **Round 4:** K all sts

☐ **Round 5:** P all sts

☐ **Round 6:** K all sts

☐ **Round 7:** P all sts

☐ **Round 8:** K all sts

4. Now you bind off (BO) half of the stitches for the front of the backpack. The stitches that remain are used to knit the flap. BO 36 sts. K the remaining sts. You will have 36 sts left when you finish the row.

5. To make the flap, K all rows until the flap is 10 inches (25.5 cm) long. You will notice a texture change because you are now knitting garter stitch.

6. BO 36 sts.

7. To begin finishing your backpack, turn the bag inside out, flatten the tube so that the flap is flat across the back of the pack, and whip stitch the bottom edges together.

8. Twisted cords are used for the straps and drawstrings of the backpack. Make two fat twisted cords using six pieces of yarn for each cord. Each piece of yarn should be 5 yards (4.5 m) long.

9. Make a knot 6 inches (15 cm) from the nonfolded ends. Untwist these tails and let them be fringe. Thread a tapestry needle with yarn and sew one fringe end to one corner of the bottom of the bag. Lay the bag flat, with the front facing down, and find the center top edge; place marker (PM) between the second and third garter-stitch ridges. Insert the folded end of the cord into the mark from the outside to the inside. Weave this cord in and out around the top edge (between the second and third garter-stitch ridges) until you get to the center on the front side.

10. Repeat step 9 with the remaining cord on the other side of the bag.

11. Cinch the top closed and tie the cord ends. Ready for use!

Funky Flip-Flops

Tickle your tootsies with these fabulous flip-flops. Make them for your whole swim team or for your next slumber party.

Size
Doesn't matter

What You Need
- Flip-flops (in your size)
- 50 yards (46 m) worsted weight yarn (I used Plymouth Encore #1382 yarn, Crystal Palace Fizz #9220.)
- Fuzzy yarn
- Flower appliqué
- Knitting needles size US #10 (6 mm)
- Safety pin
- Scissors
- Tape measure
- Tapestry needle

Gauge
Doesn't matter

Skills You'll Use
- Cast On (page 12)
- Knit Stitch (page 14)
- Stockinette Stitch (page 70)
- Bind Off (page 15)
- Whip Stitch (page 22)
- Weave In Ends (page 16)

These flip-flops are made from Plymouth Encore #2940 and Brazillia Color #0106 yarns, and a butterfly appliqué.

What You Do

1. Measure the length of the top of the flip-flop strap, starting at one end where it connects to the sole, around the top to the toe, and down the other strap. Write that number here _____.

2. You are beginning with the length and will knit the width of the strap. With your worsted weight yarn, cast on (CO) enough stitches (sts) so they will stretch on your needle to equal the above measurement.

3. Work in stockinette stitch (st st). After every few rows, check to see if the knitting will fit around the flip-flop strap.

4. When the knitting will fit around the flip-flop strap, bind off (BO) and leave a long tail (about 36 inches [92 cm] long).

5. Repeat steps 2 through 4 to make a second knitted strip.

6. To begin finishing the flip-flop, fold one strip in half lengthwise and mark the middle of the knitted piece.

7. Pin the middle of the strip to the toe piece of one flip-flop strap.

8. Thread your tapestry needle with the long tail you created when you did the bind off.

(continued on next page)

 Picture Place

Photograph your friends in their personalized knit flip-flops! Tape the photos in the Picture Place for this chapter.

For these, I used Plymouth Encore #1382 and Trendsetter Aura #8281.

9. Fold the strip around the flip-flop strap. Whip stitch the cast-on and bind-off edges together on the underside of the flip-flop. When you get to the middle, skip past the toe part and continue on the other side.

10. Tie a knot to keep your sewing from coming undone. Weave the needle back in the work a little bit to hide the end.

11. Weave in the cast-on tail.

12. Repeat steps 6 through 11 for the other flip-flop. Your personalized pair is ready for wear.

Journaling

When I host a knitting slumber party, I'll...

....

....

....

....

....

Weaving & Ribbing

Button-On E-Holster

Rompin' Round Hat

Hot Handwarmies

Basket Weave Scarf

Ribbed Leg Warmers

This is YOUR scrapbooking space. Do what you want!

Picture Place

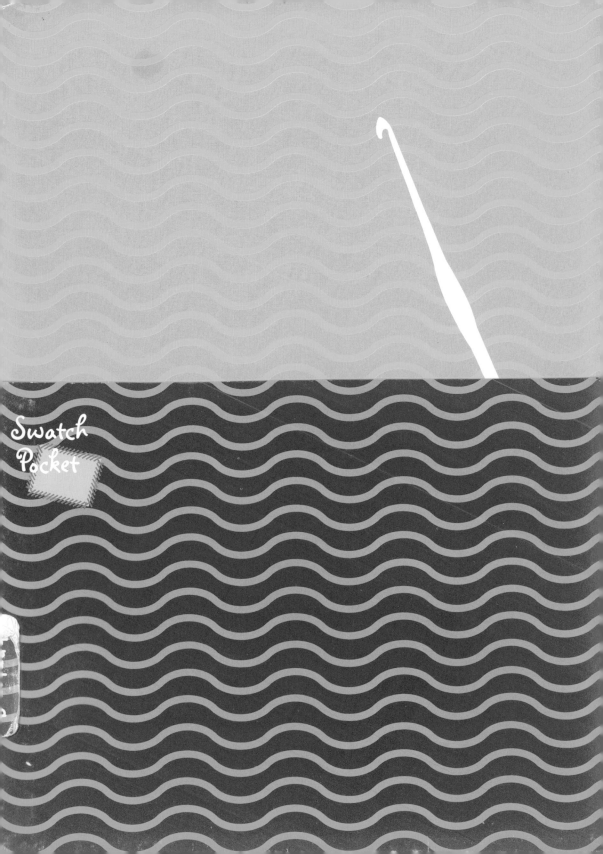

Swatch
Pocket

Chapter 6

Weaving & Ribbing

Now that you can knit and purl, why not try some new stitch combinations to create fabulous items that feel as good as they look? I'm talking about raised patterns that you see on lots of fancy sweaters and scarves. Use these skills to make a snug hat, thick fingerless gloves, and more. The project patterns begin on page 85.

Here are some tips to help you when you're knitting knit and purl stitches in the same row:

Before you start a stitch, make sure your yarn is in the proper position.

When moving from a knit stitch to a purl stitch, move your yarn to the front of the work between your needles. You also have to move your yarn to the back of the work before you do a knit stitch. (If you forget to do this, you will create an extra loop on your needle that is called a yarn over. You'll learn that technique in Chapter 7, but it won't work for these projects.)

Purl Two Together

Purl two together is a kind of **decreasing** technique. That means you dramatically reduce the number of stitches in a row to create a special effect called **ribbing**. You do it exactly as you do the knit two together technique you learned in Chapter 2, except you are purling the two stitches together.

Give it a try! Grab a piece of knitting with the last row still on the needle and enough yarn to complete at least one more row.

(A)

1. Insert the tip of the right needle into both the first and second stitches on the left needle as if to purl. Ⓐ

2. Wrap the yarn around the top (right) needle and, with the right needle, draw the yarn through both stitches. Ⓑ

(B)

3. Slide the right needle to the right until the first and second stitches on the left needle move completely off the needle. You've just completed your first purl two together.

4. Finish knitting the remaining stitches in the usual way.

5. Count the stitches on your row. Notice you have one less stitch than before. You've successfully decreased. You're ready to move on to the projects in this chapter.

Button-On E-Holster

Attach your MP3 player, phone, or handheld game to your belt loop, purse, or backpack. In style!

Size

2 inches (5 cm) wide and 5 inches (13 cm) long

What You Need

- 50 yards (45.5 m) worsted weight yarn (I used Alchemy Yarns Lone Star #42C Air & Fire.)
- Knitting needles size US #8 (5 mm)
- ½-inch (1.5-cm) button (I used a button from Geddes Studio.)
- Scissors
- Tape measure
- Tapestry needle

Gauge

4 stitches (sts) = 1 inch (2.5 cm)

Skills You'll Use

- Cast On (page 12)
- Knit Stitch (page 14)
- Purl Stitch (page 68)
- Stockinette Stitch (page 70)
- Bind Off (page 15)
- Mattress Stitch (page 71)
- Weave In Ends (page 16)

What You Do

1. Start at the top edge of the holster and knit the length. Cast on (CO) 12 stitches (sts).

2. Now knit a rib pattern stitch. To do this, knit 3 (K 3), purl 2 (P 2), for 2 inches (5 cm).

3. Time to create the middle section. Work in stockinette stitch (st st) for 6 inches (15 cm).

4. Make the other top edge. Work in K 2, P 2 rib pattern for 2 inches (5 cm).

5. Bind off (BO) 8 sts. (You will have 3 sts left on your left needle and 1 st on the right needle)

6. K the last 3 sts.

7. K each row until the skinny piece measures 6 inches (15 cm).

8. BO 4 stitches (sts).

9. To finish your e-holster, fold the piece in half so both ribbing ends meet. Sew the sides together, using the mattress stitch.

10. Weave in the ends.

11. Sew a button on the front corner, opposite the handle. One e-holster, ready for service.

Journaling

This e-holster is great for carrying music, a phone, or games. I'll use it for...

....

....

....

....

Rompin' Round Hat

Bad weather? Bad hair? Whatever! You won't need a reason to wear this hat.

Size
Fits most youth

What You Need
- 75 yards (68.5 m) bulky weight yarn (I used Felis #12.)
- 16-inch (40-cm) circular knitting needle size US #11 (8 mm)
- 4 double pointed knitting needles US #11 (8 mm)
- Scissors
- Stitch marker
- Tape measure
- Tapestry needle

Gauge
4 stitches (sts) = 1 inch (2.5 cm) in rib pattern

Skills You'll Use
- Cast On (page 12)
- Joining in the Round (page 46)
- Knit Stitch (page 14)
- Purl Stitch (page 68)
- Knitting with Double Pointed Needles (page 47)
- Knit Two Together (page 38)
- Purl Two Together (page 84)
- Bind Off (page 15)
- Weave In Ends (page 16)

What You Do

1. Begin at the bottom edge of the hat. Cast on (CO) 60 stitches (sts).

2. Join in the round, being careful not to twist, and place marker (PM) so you can identify the beginning of the round.

3. You're going to knit a **rib pattern stitch**. To do this, knit in the round: knit 3 (K 3), purl 2 (P 2). Repeat to make ribbing. Work the rib pattern stitch until your piece measures 7 inches (18 cm).

4. Change to your double pointed needles so the decreasing will go smoothly. Put 15 sts on the first needle, put 15 sts on the second needle, and put 20 sts on the third needle.

5. Shape the top of the hat by working decreases as follows:

   ☐ **Round 1:** *Knit two together (K2tog), K 1, P 2; repeat from * until you get back to the PM (40 sts remain)

   ☐ **Round 2:** *K 2, purl two together (P2tog); repeat from * until you get back to the PM (30 sts remain) .

   ☐ **Round 3:** *K2tog, P 1; repeat from * until you get back to the PM (20 sts remain)

   ☐ **Round 4:** *K2tog, K 1, P 1; repeat from * until you get back to the PM (15 sts remain)

   ☐ **Round 5:** *K2tog, P 1; repeat from * until you get back to the PM (10 sts remain)

6. Now close the top of the hat like a drawstring. Cut your yarn from the ball leaving a 10-inch (25.5-cm) tail. Thread this yarn onto your tapestry needle. Hold the needle with the stitches in your left hand. Insert the tapestry needle into the next stitch from right to left (as if you were going to purl) and take it off the knitting needle. Repeat this with each stitch until they are all on your thread. Cinch it up tight. Insert the tapestry needle into the tiny center hole of your hat and pull it to the inside.

7. Weave in all ends. Try on your hat.

Worksheet

When I'm making the decreases in this hat, the ribbing changes. It starts with K 3, P 2. On my first decrease round, it changes to _____. On my next decrease round, it changes to _____. Then it changes to _____.

The final decrease round changes the ribbing to _____.

88

Hot
Handwarmies

Keep your hands warm and your fingers free in these chic fingerless gloves.

Size

Fits most youth

What You Need

- 75 yards (68.5 m) worsted weight yarn (I used Rio De LaPlata #M66.)
- Knitting needles size US #9 (5.5 mm)
- Scissors
- Tape measure
- Tapestry needle

Gauge

3 stitches (sts) = 1 inch (2.5 cm) in knit 2, purl 2 (K 2, P 2) rib pattern

Skills You'll Use

- Cast On (page 12)
- Knit Stitch (page 14)
- Purl Stitch (page 68)
- Bind Off (page 15)
- Mattress Stitch (page 71)
- Weave In Ends (page 16)

What You Do

1. With your main yarn, cast on (CO) 34 stitches (sts). You're beginning at the bottom edge and will knit the length.

2. Work in a knit (K) 2, purl (P) 2 rib pattern until the piece measures 7 inches (18 cm).

3. Bind off (BO) all sts.

4. Beginning at the cast-on edge, do a mattress stitch seam to join the long edges of the piece for 4 inches (10 cm). Weave in the end.

5. Make the thumb opening by sewing 1 inch (2.5 cm) farther up the edge. Continue this seam all the way to the bind-off edge. Weave in the end.

6. Repeat steps 1 through 5 for the second handwarmie. Try them on. What do you think?

▲
These are made from Brown Sheep Lamb's Pride Worsted M120 Limeade, M38 Lotus Pink, M110 Orange You Glad, and M78 Aztec Turquoise yarns. They match the leg warmers on page 93.

Journaling

I could start my own knitting group. Since it's easy to pretty much knit anywhere, anytime, we could…

· ·

· ·

· ·

Basket Weave Scarf

The raised design makes this wide scarf wonderful. It's called a basket weave because it looks like, you guessed it, a woven basket.

Size

6 inches (15 cm) wide and 40 inches (102 cm) long, without fringe

What You Need

- 100 yards (91.5 m) bulky weight yarn (I used Misty Alpaca Chunky #1600.)
- 20 yards (18.5 m) novelty yarn (I used Artful Yarns Palace #361.)
- Knitting needles size US #11 (8 mm)
- Crochet hook size J
- Scissors
- Tape measure
- Tapestry needle

Gauge

3½ sts = 1 inch (2.5 cm) in basket-weave pattern (see step 2)

Skills You'll Use

- Cast On (page 12)
- Knit Stitch (page 14)
- Purl Stitch (page 68)
- Bind Off (page 15)
- Weave In Ends (page 16)
- Fringe (page 21)

What You Do

1. Cast on (CO) 20 stitches (sts). You're starting at one end of the scarf and will knit the length.

2. Work in a basket-weave pattern as follows:

   ☐ Row 1: Knit 4 (K 4), purl 4 (P 4), K 4, P 4, K 4

   ☐ Row 2: P 4, K 4, P 4, K 4, P 4

   ☐ Rows 3 through 6: Repeat rows 1 and 2 twice.

   Note: The next row changes the pattern, so you'll start creating the opposite of what you have made so far.

   ☐ Row 7: P 4, K 4, P 4, K 4, P 4

   ☐ Row 8: K 4, P 4, K 4, P 4, K 4

   ☐ Rows 9 through 12: Repeat rows 7 and 8 two more times.

3. Repeat the previous 12 rows until your scarf measures 40 inches (102 cm), or as long as you want it.

4. Bind off (BO) all sts.

5. Weave in all ends.

6. Add fringe made from your leftover yarn. Show off your scarf.

Journaling

I've knitted so much cool stuff! The clothes and accessories I made that look best together are…

· ·

· ·

· ·

 ## Picture Place

Photograph your favorite projects. Scrapbook them in this book.

Ribbed Leg Warmers

Don't be left out in the cold without a pair of snuggly, stylish leg warmers. Just think what you could do with a fuzzy or sparkly yarn!

Size
Fits most

What You Need
- 200 yards (183 m) bulky weight yarn (I used Classic Elite Beatrice #3250.)
- Knitting needles size US #9 (5.5 mm)
- Scissors
- Tape measure
- Tapestry needle

Gauge
6 stitches (sts) = 1 inch (2.5 cm) in knit 2, purl 2 (K2, P2) rib pattern

Skills You'll Use
- Cast On (page 12)
- Knit Stitch (page 14)
- Purl Stitch (page 68)
- Bind Off (page 15)
- Weave In Ends (page 16)
- Mattress Stitch (page 69)

What You Do

1. You are beginning at the bottom edge and will knit the length. Cast on (CO) 46 stitches (sts).

2. You'll work in a knit two, purl two rib pattern stitch.

> **Row 1:** *Knit 2 (K 2), purl 2 (P 2); repeat from * across the row.

> **Row 2:** *P 2, K 2; repeat from * across the row.

Repeat these two rows to make ribbing. Knit until piece measures 11 inches (28 cm), or as long as you want.

3. Bind off (BO) all sts.

4. To finish your leg warmers, weave in all ends.

5. Fold in half so the side edges meet. Use the mattress stitch to sew the sides together. Good work.

This pair is made from Brown Sheep Lamb's Pride Bulky M120 Limeade, M38 Lotus Pink, M110 Orange You Glad, M78 Aztec Turquoise, and Crystal Palace Fizz #9224 Key Lime yarns.

Journaling

I've knitted so many projects, so many different ways! Now my favorite yarns and techniques are…

....

....

....

....

Lacy Looks, Belt Loops & More

Party Poncho

Swish, Sway, Swing Skirt

Sassy Shortie Sweater

Is this your favorite project?

Picture
Place

Chapter 7

Lacy Looks, Belt Loops & More

The **yarn over** is another increasing technique. It creates small, decorative holes in your knitting. The holes can look like lace, be used as eyelets for belt loops and buttonholes, or just add an interesting detail to whatever you knit. You'll use this skill to make the projects that begin on page 97.

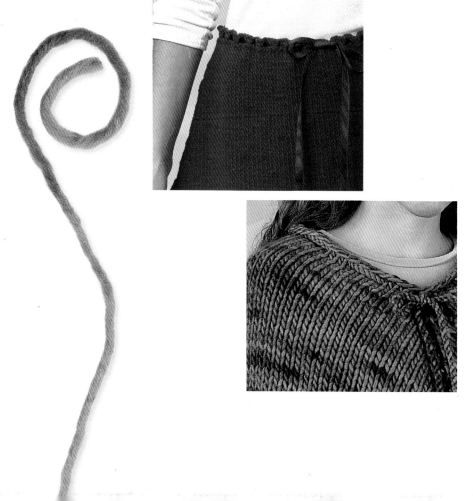

Yarn Over

To practice the yarn-over technique, you'll need a piece of knitting and the needles you've been using with that piece.

1.   Bring your yarn to the front of your work as if you are going to purl.

2.   Move the yarn to the back, passing it over the top of the right needle. This piece of yarn, over the right needle, is the yarn over. (See Ⓐ for the standard yarn over, which is how it looks when you are making knit stitches. Ⓑ shows how it looks to create a yarn over before making a purl stitch.) You have just created a yarn over, but you won't really be able to see it properly until you work the next stitch.

3.   Make a knit stitch. Look at your work carefully. See how there is an extra piece of yarn on your needle? It doesn't quite look like a knit stitch, though, does it? That's OK.

4.   On your next row, you will knit or purl this yarn over (whichever technique your pattern says). Now all your loops on your needle look like stitches. Nice work on your first yarn-over practice piece!

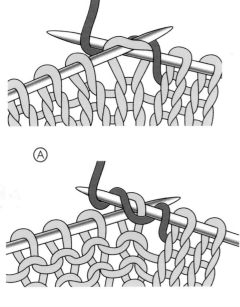

Ⓐ

Ⓑ

Journaling

If I had a limited amount of time and had to choose between knitting a few small pieces or making one big project, I …

....

....

....

Party Poncho

Who needs a holiday? You'll feel like celebrating any time you wear this fantastic fringed poncho.

Size

Fits most youth (Neck opening 9 inches (23 cm), shoulders 18 inches (46 cm), length 26 inches (66 cm). Increasing or decreasing the number of rows you knit will alter the size.)

What You Need

- 500 yards (457 m) bulky weight yarn (I used J. Knits' Felter's Dream, bulky, in the color Alabama.)
- 16-inch (40-cm) circular knitting needle size US #11 (8 mm)
- 24-inch (60-cm) circular knitting needle size US #11 (8 mm)
- Crochet hook size J
- Scissors
- 1 stitch marker
- 2 stitch markers in a second color
- Tape measure
- Tapestry needle

Gauge

3 sts (stitches) = 1 inch (2.5 cm) in garter stitch

Skills You'll Use

- Cast On (page 12)
- Joining in the Round (page 46)
- Knit Stitch (page 14)
- Yarn Over (page 96)
- Bind Off (page 15)
- Fringe (page 21)
- Twisted Cord (page 39)
- Weave In Ends (page 16)

What You Do

1. Begin at the neck of your poncho and then knit the length. Using the 16-inch (40 cm) circular needle, cast on (CO) 60 stitches (sts).

2. Place marker (PM) on the right needle and join in the round. Be careful not to twist the stitches.

3. Knit (K) 1 round.

4. K 15 sts, and PM (using the second color place marker) on the right needle. K 30 sts and PM (using the second color again). Finish the round.

Note: Take a moment to examine your knitting. At this point you have three markers on your needle. The color of your first marker is (fill in the blank) _____. This marker indicates the beginning and end of a round. You will not do increases at this marker. The color of your second and third markers is _____. These markers indicate where to make the increases.

5. Now shape your poncho as you knit the length.

☐ **Round 1 (increase):** K to the last stitch (st) before the first marker. Yarn over (YO), and then K 1. Move the marker to the right needle. YO, K to the last st before the next marker. YO, K 1. Move the marker to the right needle. YO, K to the end of the round marker. Move the marker to the right needle.

☐ **Round 2 (plain knitting):** K all sts. Move the markers to the right needle when you get to them, and keep going all the way around to the beginning of the round marker.

Repeat the increase and plain rounds until the poncho is as long as you want it. When your sts get bunched up on your needle, start using the 24-inch (60 cm) needle in your right hand until all the stitches are on the 24-inch needle (60 cm) and then only use that needle.

Note: It can get confusing about whether you are on an increase round or a plain round. You will probably want to devise a system to help you keep track of it. I say just use the check-offs to mark each round after you have completed it.

6. Bind off (BO) all stitches loosely.

7. Add fringe along your poncho edge, cutting your pieces at least 10 inches (26 cm) long.

8. Make a twisted cord for the neck with three pieces of yarn, 4 yards (4 m) each. Weave the cord in and out of the stitches around the neck. Put on your poncho and give it a twirl.

Swish, Sway, Swing Skirt

The ruffles make this ribbon-belted skirt move
with you. It's versatile, too. Wear it with boots for
a fabulous look. Be casual in flip-flops or lo tops.

Size

Skirts require more ease (room between the fabric and the body) than tops. Be sure to measure your hips and use the nearest size in the chart.

What You Need

- 400 (500, 600, 700) yards of worsted weight yarn (I used Nashua Cilantro #9 Geranium.)
- 24-inch (60 cm) circular knitting needle size US #9 (5.5 mm)
- 36-inch (90 cm) circular knitting needle size US #9 (5.5 mm)
- 2 stitch markers, each a different color
- Scissors
- Tape measure
- Tapestry needle
- 3/8-inch ribbon, 60 (64, 68, 72) inches [152.5 (162.5, 172.5, 183) cm]

Gauge

4 sts (stitches) = 1 inch (2.5 cm) in stockinette stitch

Skills You'll Use

- Cast On (page 12)
- Joining in the Round (page 46)
- Purl Stitch (page 68)
- Knit Two Together (page 38)
- Yarn Over (page 96)
- Knit Stitch (page 14)
- Knit in Front & Back of Stitch (page 60)
- Bind Off (page 15)
- Weave In Ends (page 16)

Skirt Sizing Chart

Actual Hip Measurement	28"	32"	36"	40"
Metric Equivalent	71 cm	81.5 cm	91.5 cm	101.5 cm
Finished Measurement	40"	44"	48"	52"
Metric Equivalent	81.5 cm	91.5 cm	101.5 cm	111.5 cm
# of Cast On Stitches	120	136	152	168
Knit Round for Length	11"	12.5"	13.5"	14.5"
Metric Equivalent	28 cm	32 cm	34.5 cm	37 cm
Yardage Needed	400	500	600	700

What You Do

1. You begin at the waistband and knit the length of the skirt. Using the 24-inch (60 cm) circular needle, cast on (CO) 120 (136, 152, 168) stitches (sts). Place marker (PM) and join in the round being careful not to twist. The color of my beginning of the round marker is _____.

2. Purl (P) 1 round, PM after stitch 60 (68, 76, 84). The color of my halfway marker is _____.

3. This round creates little holes, known as eyelets, for the waistband. Move the markers to the right needle when you get to them. *Knit two stitches together (K2tog), yarn over (YO), repeat from* to the end of the round.

Note: Don't forget to do the last YO at the end of the round. Because the first stitch in the next round is a purl stitch, after passing the yarn over the top of the right needle for the yarn over, bring it back between the needles and to the front into the purl position.

4. P 1 round.

5. Now you will knit and shape the length of the skirt. Move the markers to the right needle when you get to them.

☐ **Rounds 1 through 5:** Knit (K) 5 rounds.

☐ **Round 6:** Knit in the front and the back of the stitch (kf&b), knit to 2 sts before the next marker, kf&b, k 1, kf&b, knit to 2 stitches before the next marker, kf&b, k 1.

Repeat these six rounds nine more times. After each increase round, you will have four more stitches. After your final increase round you will have 160 (176, 192, 208) sts.

6. Knit rounds until piece measures 11 (12½, 13½, 14½) inches [28 (32, 34.5, 37) cm] (or desired length).

This skirt is made from Plymouth Cotton #9002 yarn.

7. Use your 36-inch needle in your right hand and P 1 round. This way your needle will be long enough to hold all the stitches for the ruffle, which you knit next.

8. Increasing after every stitch creates the ruffle. *K1, YO, repeat from * to the end of the round. Don't forget the last YO at the end of the round. You have just doubled your stitch count. (That's a good thing.)

9. P all rounds until the ruffle measures 2¾ inches (7 cm).

10. Make the ruffle longer.

☐ **Round 1:** K 1 round.

☐ **Round 2:** P 1 round.

Repeat these two rounds one more time.

11. Loosely bind off (BO) all sts and weave in all ends.

12. Weave the ribbon in and out of the eyelets at the waistband and tie a bow in front.

Picture Place

Try on your skirt. Strike a pose and have a friend take your picture! Scrapbook it on the divider for this chapter.

Sassy Shortie Sweater

Check out the see-through arm seams and textured trim on this shrug.

Size

Fits chest measuring 28 (32, 36) inches [71 (81.5, 91.5) cm]

What You Need

- 400 yards (366 m) of worsted weight yarn (I used Jade Sapphire Mongolian Cashmere in the color #19 Robin's Egg.)
- Knitting needles
- 24-inch (60-cm) circular knitting needle size US #8 (5 mm)
- 4 double pointed needles size US #8 (5 mm)
- Scissors
- Stitch markers
- Tape measure
- Tapestry needle

Gauge

4 sts (stitches) = 1 inch (2.5 cm) in stockinette stitch

Skills You'll Use

- Cast On (page 12)
- Knit Stitch (page 14)
- Purl Stitch (page 68)
- Stockinette Stitch (page 70)
- Yarn Over (page 96)
- Knitting with Double Pointed Needles (page 47)
- Bind Off (page 15)
- Weave In Ends (page 16)

What You Do

This sweater is knitted with a special technique called Top Down. As the name suggests, you will begin at the neck edge. Then you will add stitches every other row. These stitches are added in the body area and also in the sleeve area. It is fun to watch it grow as you knit it. The best part about knitting sweaters this way is that you don't have to sew any seams when you are finished.

1. You start at the neck edge and will knit the shortie from the top down. Using the circular needle, cast on (CO) 65 stitches (sts).

2. First you will knit the collar ribbing.

☐ **Row 1:** Knit (K) 3, *K 1, Purl (P) 1, repeat from *, end with K 4.

☐ **Row 2:** K 3, *P 1, K 1, repeat from *, end with P 1, K 3.

Repeat these two rows three more times.

3. Divide the piece into sections and begin the **raglan shaping**, which is what will build your sleeves. You will use four stitch markers to separate the piece into five sections (right front, right sleeve, back, left sleeve, and left front). One marker is placed between the right front and right sleeve, one is placed between the right sleeve and back, one is placed between the back and left sleeve, and the last is placed between the left sleeve and left front. (You might find it helpful to have someone read this to you, one step at a time, so you don't get lost between the directions and your knitted piece.) K 11, Yarn over (YO), place marker (PM), K 1, YO, K 9, YO, PM, K 1, YO, K 21, YO, PM, K 1, YO, K 9, YO, PM, K 1, YO, K 11 (73 sts).

Note: Because of the placement of the markers, the sleeve sections do not have equal stitch counts; the same is true for the front sections.

(continued on next page)

4. Increase the number of sts to make the piece large enough to go around the shoulders.

☐ **Row 1:** K 3, purl (P) to the last 3 stitches, K 3.

☐ **Row 2:** *Knit to the marker, YO, slip marker, K 1, YO, repeat from * 3 more times then knit to the end of the row (81 sts).

5. Now you will remove the sleeve stitches from the knitting needles so you can knit them later. Thread your tapestry needle with a 24-inch (60 cm) piece of scrap yarn. Set it aside. Cut another piece of scrap yarn 24 inches (60 cm) long. Knit to the first marker. Take the marker off your needle. Move all the stitches between the first and second marker onto the scrap yarn by inserting the tapestry needle from right to left into each stitch and removing it from the knitting needle. When you get to the next stitch marker, remove it from the needle.

6. Knit the next stitches on the left needle until you to get the next stitch marker. Remove the stitch marker. Move all the stitches until the next marker onto the scrap yarn by inserting the tapestry needle into each stitch and removing it from the knitting needle. When you get to the next stitch marker, remove it from the needle. Knit the remaining stitches. You should have 113 (129, 145) sts remaining on the needle and 44 (52, 60) sts on each piece of scrap yarn.

7. Continue knitting the body of the sweater.

☐ **Row 1:** K 3, P to last 3 stitches, K 3.

☐ **Row 2:** Knit all stitches.

Repeat these two rows for 2 inches (5 cm) more or desired length.

8. Finish lower edge with ribbing.

☐ **Row 1:** K 3, *K 1, P 1, repeat from *, end with K 4.

☐ **Row 2:** K 3, *P 1, K 1, repeat from *, end with P 1, K 3.

Repeat these two rows eight more times.

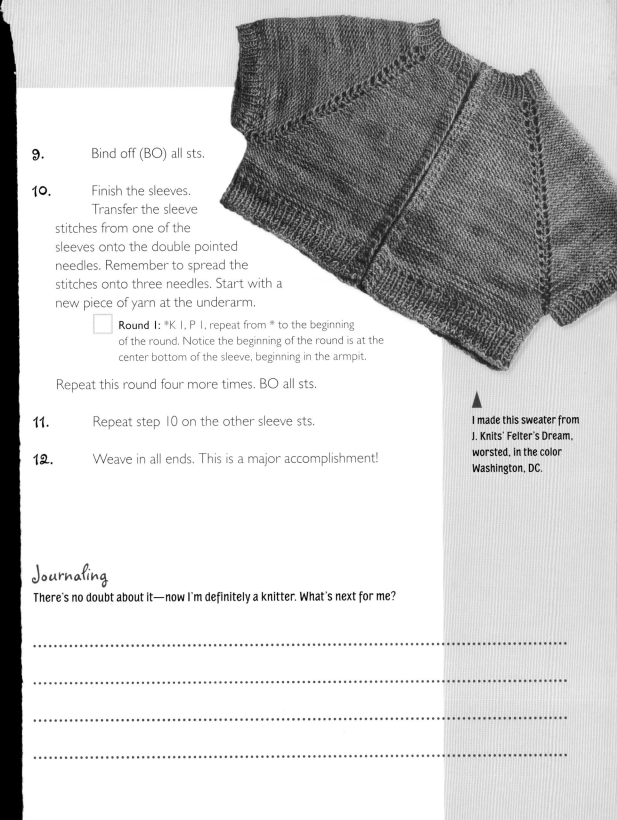

9. Bind off (BO) all sts.

10. Finish the sleeves. Transfer the sleeve stitches from one of the sleeves onto the double pointed needles. Remember to spread the stitches onto three needles. Start with a new piece of yarn at the underarm.

> **Round 1:** *K 1, P 1, repeat from * to the beginning of the round. Notice the beginning of the round is at the center bottom of the sleeve, beginning in the armpit.

Repeat this round four more times. BO all sts.

11. Repeat step 10 on the other sleeve sts.

12. Weave in all ends. This is a major accomplishment!

▲
I made this sweater from J. Knits' Felter's Dream, worsted, in the color Washington, DC.

Journaling

There's no doubt about it—now I'm definitely a knitter. What's next for me?

....

....

....

....

Uh-Oh!

Almost everything I knit has a few mistakes in it. If a mistake will drastically change the final project, like having twice or half as many stitches as I'm supposed to, I fix it. Having just one or two bad stitches isn't a big deal. No one but you will ever know about mistakes that small. Read on for uh-oh fixes.